Traces in Blood, Bone, & Stone

Also by Loonfeather Press

Stories Migrating Home:
A Collection of Anishinaabe Prose

Traces in Blood, Bone, & Stone

Contemporary Ojibwe Poetry

Kimberly M. Blaeser, Editor

Loonfeather Press
Bemidji, Minnesota

First printing 2006
Printed in Canada by Hignell Book Printing
ISBN 0-926147-17-X

This publication is printed on 100 percent recycled material including
20 percent post-consumer waste. This acid-free paper is oxygen-bleached,
an environmentally friendly process.

Loonfeather Press is a not-for-profit small press organized under section
501 (c) (3) of the United States Internal Revenue Code.

This publication is made possible, in part, by the Region 2 Arts Council
through funding from the McKnight Foundation.

Loonfeather Press
P.O. Box 1212
Bemidji, MN 56619

For our ancestors and elders,
whose voices and histories imbue the spirit of these poems.

For our children and grandchildren,
to whom we pass both words and spirit.

Acknowledgments

The gathering of these poems has taken place over a number of years and many have contributed to the anthology. I thank Betty Rossi and Loonfeather Press for their dedication to regional and especially to Native writing, and to the Region 2 Arts Council for grant funding. We are honored and grateful to have the work of Joe Geshick for our cover and I thank both Joe and LeeAnn for making this possible. I owe a debt to many of the contributors and to friends and colleagues who over the years have introduced me to many new Ojibwe writers. I thank Karen Strom whose work on my web site uncovered "ex-patriot" Anishinaabe writers from various spots in the Americas, several of whom have work in this volume. Miigwech to you all for these connections. I am grateful to my research assistants Beth Bretl and Diane Unterweger who worked on correspondence and manuscript compilation. And, as always, I am grateful to my husband, Len Wardzala, who offered various kinds of technical assistance and endless encouragement. Finally, I must offer my biggest thank you to my children, Gavin and Amber Dawn, for earnestness and innocence, for love in all circumstances, for loud and appropriate interference. They are my constant reminders of why we do this work.

I thank the editors of the following publications in which some of these works originally appeared, sometimes in a slightly different form:

"Outside White Earth" previously appeared in *Songs from this Earth on Turtle's Back*; "How Soon" in the *North Dakota Quarterly*; "The Failure of Certain Charms" in the *Mid-American Review*; "Dodem Dream Song" in *Returning the Gift*; "Rockin' Chair Lady," "At Geronimo's Grave," "Bear," "Blueberries," "Drum Song," "Fish Tale," and "Creation Story" in *At Geronimo's Grave* by Armand Garnet Ruffo; "Center of Gravity," "Mapping the Land," "Indian War," and "Red Dogs in the Heat" in *Nitaawichige: Anishinaabe Poetry & Prose*; "Songs for Discharming" in *Songs for Discharming*; "Zen and Woman's Way of Parking" in *Days of Obsidian, Days of Grace*; "Dancing the Rounds" and "Tossing Around" in *Native Poets in Canada: A Contemporary Anthology*; "stray bullets" from *my heart is a stray bullet* by kateri akiwenzie-damm; "Family Tree" in *Imaginary (Re-) Locations;* "your old lost loves," "Haiku Seasons" and "Recite the Names of All the Suicided Indians" from *Absentee Indians and Other Poems* by Kimberly Blaeser; "Where I Was That Day" and "Rewriting Your Life" from *Trailing You* by Kimberly Blaeser; "Apprenticed to Justice" in *Valparaiso Poetry Review;* "Tangerine Light" from *Uncombed Hair;* "True Myth" in *Fishing for Myth,* New Rivers Press, 1997; "Offering: First Rice," "Nesting Dolls," "Vermillion Hands," "Offering: Ojibwe" and "Poem for Our Ojibwe Names" © Heid Erdrich, from *The Mother's Tongue,* Cambridge: Salt Publishing, 2005. Reprinted with permission of the publisher; "Indian Boarding School: The Runaways," "Captivity," "Shelter," "Turtle Mountain Reservation" and "The Red Sleep of Beasts" from *Jacklight* by Louise Erdrich; "The Sacraments" from *Baptism of Desire* by Louise Erdrich; "Spring Evening on Blind Mountain" and "Morning Fire" from *Original Fire* by Louise Erdrich; "The Refugees," "Saint Bernard," "Everything You Need to Know in Life You Learned at Boarding School," "Grandmother in Indian School" and "Chi-Ko-ko-koho-and the Boarding School Prefect" from *Nitaawichige;* "To the Woman Who Just Bought a Set of Native American Spirituality Dream Interpretation Cards" in *Sister Nations;* "Nindaniss Wawashkeshikwesens on a Winter Night" in *My Home as I Remember;* "In Neah Bay," "Prayer Bowl," "Poem for Patrick Eller," "Jailer" and "Blue Horses" from *Spirit Horses* by Al Hunter; "The Blue Apache" and "Litany II" are reprinted with permission of Spirit Bear Publishing, Minneapolis/Chicago; "Shrinking Away," "Manoomin," "Lifetime of Sad," "Wahbegan," "Ogichidaa" and "Wiigwass" from *Walking the Rez Road* by Jim Northrup; "Gravity" and "Visitation" from *Exploding Chippewas* by Mark Turcotte; "Flies Buzzing," "Cyrus Calls for His Pony" and "Hands" from *The Feathered Heart* by Mark Turcotte; "Rambo to Flambeau" and "Not on the Guest List," from *Powwows, Fat Cats, and Other Indian Tales* by E. Donald Two-Rivers; "Family Photograph" and "seven woodland crows" in *Voices of the Rainbow;* "Hail Stones" from *Seventeen Chirps* by Gerald Vizenor; "fat green flies" and "plum blossoms" from *Matsushima* by Gerald Vizenor.

The title of this publication, *Traces in Blood, Bone, & Stone,* was taken from Vizenor's poem, "almost ashore."

Contents

About Our Contributors

The Voice That Speaks

Kimberly Blaeser

We begin with a cry, a hunger large or small that opens our newborn mouths. An instinct to wail or suck. Our vigorous tiny mouths latch to the sweet drip of our history. We milk our past, swallow, and grow our new bodies.

The poetry of contemporary Ojibwe writers ranges richly over a wide sweep of experiences. The poets in this collection live in Canada, in Minnesota, Michigan, Wisconsin, Washington, and California, on reserves and reservations, in urban communities. They are by trade or devotion teachers, activists, college professors, parents, artists, and professional writers. They are Native Language speakers, English-only speakers, and every variation in between. Some are baby boomers, some veterans of foreign wars.

But despite these many differences in origin and experience of the authors, some threads of similarity run through the works. Many of the poems weave with their lines and stanzas a connection to the tribal histories of the Ojibwe nations. Turtle Mountain. Red Lake. White Earth. Cape Croker. They carry an awareness of the historical struggles of the mass of Indian people of the Americas. Speak a litany of the losses wrought through treaties, boarding and residential schools, and military occupations. In verse and free verse they trace the strength of our survivals as they hold a devotion for what has passed. In the weft and warp of their telling, the authors map relationships with the landscapes that house these histories, sketch the community of natural places and creatures. Ultimately, they voice a path for continuance. Many of the poems gesture beyond themselves to the mythic and ceremonial realities of the Ojibwe people. To tricksters, windigos, and earth divers. To sacred tobacco and harvest rituals. They carry the sounds of dual-languages and multiple dialects, the memories and stories of several generations, the dreams of many beyond the writers. Thus they are multi-vocal, layered in sense and meaning, marked by allusion to something beyond the words, imbued with a timelessness and intergenerational reality.

At the same time, the thirty-plus writers represented in this collection fill their poems with the details of the everyday, the contemporary quandaries and experiences of the authors. Denise Sweet writes of "Zen and Woman's Way of Parking." Armand Garnet Ruffo looks with wonder at the American commercialization of culture in the Sante Fe "current of silver and turquoise." Can contemporary Ojibwe poetry straddle both the mythic and the post-modern? If the poems or the writers refuse the simple stereotypic roles and poses carved for Indians and Indian Literature of the Americas, they accomplish this partly through a delicious ironic humor, partly through the dissolution and outstripping of the mere literary. The personae in Linda LeGarde Grover's "The Refugees" claims identification with "the other Indians / not the New Age beauties you watch on made-for-TV movies." The ice sculpture in Gordon Henry's "How Soon" transforms into a pool of water, not by mystery but by nature. The poem itself dissolves as the reader enters into the experience of cycle more real than the words that drew her there. These poems are more than literature; they are tactile traces—in blood, bone, and stone.

In one way or another these native authors are engaged in teaching the tenuous art of survival. Jim Northrup's autobiographical stand-in learns in "Shrinking Away" that white professionals or institutions can't cure him of PTSD and he tells us: "surviving the peace was up to me." When Heid Erdrich's poem "Vermillion Hands" requests "Teach me back into time / Until I know there is no time," the longing voiced is for a connection through the "red ochre" pictographs, not just to the past or to cultural knowledge, but to the endurance they represent. When the poems overlay descriptions of barrooms, rez dogs, or the Native American dream cards of contemporary experience with chants in Ojibwemowin, animal spirits, or tribal memories, an imagistic combustion takes place. As readers we are left with traces of the cultural reality of the contemporary Anishinaabeg.

The voice that speaks learns language new each day, traces with its tongue all things within reach. In mouths whose cheeks are puffed, full of the collective rage and memory, words cannot be stifled. These songs seep out the edges even as we sleep. So strong our voice, we carve with our breath.

Note on the use of Anishinaabemowin or the Ojibwe language: Because of variations in regional dialects and the use of different systems of orthography, spellings may vary. In all instances, we have kept the spelling employed by the author. In determining whether or not to offer a translation for non-English words, we have again followed the original text since this latter decision may reflect a political stance on the part of the writer. Several standard Ojibwe dictionaries are available for readers who are unfamiliar with the language and find the meaning unclear from context. (See, for example, *A Concise Dictionary of Minnesota Ojibwe* assembled by John D. Nichols and Earl Nyholm or *Ojibway Language Lexicon* created by Basil Johnston.)

Traces in Blood, Bone, & Stone

kateri akiwenzie-damm

stray bullets

my touch is a history book
full of lies and half-forgotten truths
written by others
who hold the pens
and power

my heart is a stray bullet
ricocheting in an empty room

my head was sold
for the first shiny trinket
offered

my beliefs were bought cheap
like magic potions at a traveling road show
with promises
everyone wants to believe
but only a fool invests in

my name was stolen
by bandits in black robes
my world was taken
for a putting green

night falling woman

this is as it was meant to be
for if one footstep misplaced i might have
walked past someone at some other table
brushed against some other arm or knee and found myself
walking backwards at daybreak instead of counting the moons i found
when your hand touching my arm opened a hole in the sky
and i jumped or was pushed or was pulled

and i keep falling

hummingbirds hovering turn translucent
bats diving fireflies a token sign of life's lesser gods
lighting the trail of tears you once cried
for all the displaced people who come true in you
she who is born of many grandparents

now makinak and negik medicine i gift you
blue clay seemah cedar sweetgrass and me
while marten bearing the weight of other-being
sleeps and dreams

be still

in your arms the weary traveler finds shelter
by you the hungry are nourished
and though dodem says we are not kin
we wander like sisters walking twin planets
though you move as though music fires your soul
while i stumble graceless as a newborn doe struggling
to her feet

but nothing in life is reasonable not life itself
nor the trajectory of running that leads us home again
so who can say we don't share the same blood
or that you are not the child of a dream
i imagined several lifetimes ago?

here time swallows its own tail and our spirits laughing
recall Shawnee chief and Muskoke leader fixing the morning star
two horses breaking free a battlefield of brilliant red berries returning
  ever turning
towards daybreak waking two fireflies escaping and it is here
and i know you beyond logic or a singe lifetime
remembering with each falling star that moment
your touch broke open
the sky i fall into

the rez: a still life

otis listening to jazz
pietra calls him "a layabout"
doesn't matter, he's half asleep
got the munchies
got nothing to eat

rez life takes a toll
always the damn spring rain
flooding and mudding
the dirt roads
truck always needing a wash
someone always looking for cash
some kid always looking for a place to crash

nobody forgets
a damn thing

even the dogs chase your shadows

man, you don't get away with anything

life on the rez: kinda like being in jail
(more indians here than you can shake a nightstick at!)
except for the water rocks and trees
except for those coyote tracks
and the buzzards circling

except that you love it

it's a life sentence

even if you wanted to leave
this land would never let you go
too many bones singing you home
too many kids at your heels

but ask the bearclaw woman
with the fistprint markings running up her trunk
ask her about the difference between roots
and marked territory

anyways there's hope

you might get paroled
find a shelter maybe
maybe you'll invent new ways to break out
take a gun or knife or rope pull a mcgyver and form a key

but like the song says cuz
you can check out but you can't ever leave

still life on the rez ain't so bad
where else are you gonna see your history in the patterns of stars
or read the changing seasons like a story
where else are you gonna complain without it being an act of treason
or eat fry bread and hangover soup with your 12 stepping cousins
where else are you gonna pick fiddleheads, drink sap from a bucket
laugh with the aunties or tell dirty jokes in the kitchen
where else can you be sure no one's gonna assume you're a storyteller
just 'cause you're an indian writer from ontario

where else is sex between indians just good gossip
but not the least bit shocking?

otis doesn't care about any of this
he still hasn't got a thing to eat

he looks out at the rain
curls up and falls asleep

Benae anami-auzoowin

Baeshoowitiwishin
K'zaugi-in
K'd'mindo-waewaemin

Babaum-itoowishin
Ae-izhi-anami-auziyaun
Medawaewae-aungissaeyaun

Maewishkoohnssing
Kbaubee-in
K'zaugi-in

Baeshoowitiwishin
K'd'mindo-waewaemin
K'zaugi-in

Translation Basil Johnston,

partridge song

come to me
my love
i am calling

hear my song
sweet one
i am drumming

in the reeds
dear one
i am waiting

come to me
my love
i am calling

W'ae-anami-auzoot Naunoogishkauhnse

Tibishko nau-noogishkauhnse
Ae-izhi-mino-waugumminik
Waubugonae-oohnzibun
Mee ae-izhi-maudagaezim-aendumawn
Tchi zaugi-in

Translation Basil Johnston

hummingbird song

there is a hummingbird
caught in my throat
waiting to taste
the sweet nectar
of your body
in full bloom

Nindo-waewaemauh Ishkotae-benaessih

N'cheebitauk-doonaewutch; tibishko
Anaukunushkook zhaushaub-waukishinoowaut gooning
Yaushkawaewae-ishkauwaut; mee ae-izhi
Gauskawaewaeminaun
Kissin-aunimuk

Tipaubauwizhishin
Tipaubauwizhishin

N'cheeby-tauk-anikae
Nkunimun zagazoowaeitaenoon
Nweeyoowim inautaeshimooh
Keen nakae
Bunu-inaeniminaun

Tipaubauwizhishin
Tipaubauwizhishin

Naunauwi-zeepeengawae
Iskutae-tigawaeyauh
Bunaussin mitauwun
Nindo-naewautoot
Oshki-zeepeekaun
Tchi aundji-igiyaun

Tipaubauwizhishin
Tipaubauwizhishin

N'zaugaidjinaewiss
Pushkawau-dauwingauh
Weesigau-kummikau
Bawaussin
Baussi-kummikauh

Tipaubauwizhishin
Tipaubauwizhishin

Translation Basil Johnston

kateri akiwenzie-damm

calling thunderbird

my lips are dry
reeds piercing late winter snow
rattling your name
in the cold wind blasting
from my lungs

rain into me, love
rain into me

my arms are dry
bones bereft of marrow
this flesh is a shadow
stretching toward your body
brittle so brittle your memory

rain into me, love
rain into me

my eyes are dry
riverbeds cracked by the sun
dust settling in stillness
thirsting for fresh streams
to revive me

rain into me, love
rain into me

my womb is dry
earth unseeded
my soil bitter tasting
fallen
fallow

rain into me, my love
rain into me

David Beaulieu

Lost Memories

Late in the season of his mother's life John Clement sat with her to
ask her what she knew. The past was long over due and now entered the
room. History waited at the door. The insatiable silent listening of
what no longer exists waited upon the present, its stories to tell. His
father had left on a journey to yesterday, never to return. Nothing was
said about the good-bye. The memory of his father existed in his
mother's silent listening to years of what she would not say. His
face had taken on the shape of the hole of her silence. A spider web's
lace of unexpressed memories decorated the border across the rim of the
passage to the unspoken.

A card had arrived after his father left, but had since then not been
read. Reading it now she began to cry as if all the time since those
days had never gone by. The past rushed forward having stayed among
far away places to catch up to the traveler now sitting still. It arrived on
a card and in a memory that had lingered beguiled by the view.

The card had the verse of a song written to say good-by, a song that
had been sung in a heart long ago; "come back to me." A melody of
memories fell with her tears into the emptiness of the shadows of what
was never said. His face appeared in the mirrored reflection of her long
silence. She touched his cheek.

Some memories never return, never able to find their way back. Having
lingered too long they are forever lost among the places of their origin
leaving us behind. The blue longing of the ocean. Boats of memories
forever afloat with no shore in sight. To see what others have seen, what
others have remembered gives life back to life and blue back to blue.

John Clement would go there where his father had lived among the lost memories. Through that hole of silence in search of all that was not said he would go. As he entered the silence the wind emerged, forming a cyclone around the hole. The cold winter wind, the icy breath of the past, whispered an untold longing to behold. He looked into the middle of the passage to what used to be, which expanded and grew. The wind shifted to push him forward, ever forward into the insatiable silent abyss. When the wind stopped blowing, his mother stopped crying and would say no more. The doorway to long ago slammed shut leaving only the echo of her silent memory to fill the room. John Clement was gone.

Alice Bird

Three Stories

I

In their wisdom
the old people told me:
Do not let the doctors with their razor
sharp knives touch the spider
For they will startle him and awake
him from his slumber.

Now the spider has made another web.
Though they burn him out,
In fury he will return
to get his revenge
Devouring everything in his path.

II

George said all I want is a good price
for my muskrats, beaver, wolverine,
fox, and martin pelts
to buy bright cloth for the wives.

The storekeeper does not understand.
He wants to throw me out.
Now he lies in a pool of blood.
In danger for my life
I make a run with my wives.
High upon the hill overlooking
two rivers I find refuge.
One wife is barren and the other
bears me twin boys.

Alice Bird

III

He takes his violin from its battered
case and begins to play.
She gets up
arms dangling from her sides.
Her feet begin to move
over the wooden planks.
It sounds like potatoes
being dumped onto the floor.
He chants: *Dance, Jessie, dance.*

Kimberly Blaeser

Family Tree

A boxer grandfather
who once fought Star Bad Boy
who sired six
beer drinking German sons
all with the same big hands.

The grandmother I never knew
who might be responsible
for the heft of my thighs
is for certain the origin
of my father's sauerkraut
and fine venison sausage
perhaps for his sweet tooth
and maybe mine, too.

My father who turned those boxer hands
to percussion and gesture
tapping and clapping and snapping
the quick-step songs
but buttercupping the fingertips
to croon on bended knee
the long drawn *Mona Lisa,*
Mona Lisa, men have loved you.

My Chippewa grandmother
who was midwife and medicine gatherer
tiny twig of a woman
who bore twelve children
bore the loss of two babies to influenza
the loss of one grown son
to white man's war
and the loss of a generation
limbo Indians turned to alcohol.

My Indian grandpa
who squints darkly
into cameras of the past
who raised two generations
on rocky-bottom allotted land
twenty-eight slow horse miles
from the village store
his crinkly story eyes
my first memory at two.

My mother born of dawn
in a reckless moon of miscegenation
whose foot rode the pedals
on fifty years of Singer sewing machines
her needles dancing rituals on a ribbon shirt
blending our jagged mismatched edges in a crazy quilt.

Kimberly Blaeser

Two uncles who ran away
from Pipestone
Indian boarding school
and an auntie who stayed
who lost her fingers
saw them caught mangled
in the laundry press
who beaded kneaded
quilted and braided
her way through four children
just the same.

Houses and fish camps full of cousins
who rotated authority
on marbles sex and skunk etiquette
whose probation blues and 49 songs
deprived me of bee stings broken bones
swimmers itch drunken despair
and suicide
in whose tangled litters
blond & black-haired softball players
I fearlessly set down
my suckling babies.

My great grandfather *Nii-Waan,*
Mii-nii-waan-noo-gwosh, Lover of Natural Things
whose Antell heart I am said to bear
who carried his name with humbleness
as I try to
and sometimes with rage
fire brown eyes sharp as any weapon
who cupped his hands around fertile seeds
brown fingers the pinecone
shelled house of protection.

All my relations.

The Womanless Wedding

He will tell you he was a mess sergeant
a square dance caller
a pile driver, pool hustler
and a poker player.
Some say he was a dandy
fancy white belts and drawers full of ties.
He may say he was a hula dancer
in a womanless wedding,
and I will believe him.

For though I have seen him sit
hand closed to strike his breast
at each peal of the Angelus bell,
lips mouthing his silent recitation,
I have seen that same hand
cupped lightly
around the puck at a shuffleboard table.
With body rocking and fingers caressing,
his hand slides that metal disc
gently floating the silver
ahead and back on the sawdust
pulling it close, then spinning it
swiftly powerfully   away
his aim sure
his arm following
and the song he hums
never stopping
until the beer glass touches his lips.

Kimberly Blaeser

So if he says he played basketball
against the Harlem Globetrotters
and won,
I know it is just possible.
Possible that the man who recites from memory
The Rime of the Ancient Mariner
has long forgotten his children's ages
and his own confirmation name.
And even if I had not seen
those black and whites
of a young blond man
holding a koala bear,
I would not doubt his stories
of New Guinea and Australia
nor his account of malaria
and coming home to another man's baby.

Too often I have watched
those tired blue eyes
stare through the pinprick holes of age
struggling to find coins, silverware,
door handles, the washroom;
trying hard to recognize faces,
to sort ones from twenties,
the lost dead from the living,
searching sometimes in desperation
to recall the wildest, the sweetest,
the most familiar legends from another century
of the boy who skipped three grades
in the white clapboard country school,
of the man who fed me Rocky Mountain oysters
and gave my dog beer.

Mornings that man sits
nothing but coffee for company.
But ninety years is time enough
and I won't begrudge him
a womanless wedding
and other contradictions.

Kimberly Blaeser

your old lost loves

for I have left
the same handsome men
standing in photos
with that girl
from my past
seeing them grow younger
leaner, taller
each year
hearing their deep
fine words
in the rustle
of each fall's leaves

together
barefoot
we walk
country roads
ankle deep in mud
I turn to you
young laughing ghost
hubba hubba
never quite matching
your daring
ooh la la
I need those memories
fourteen kids
and no papa

some lovers I know
in stories
some by heart
for I stand
just as you did
on the same lake shore
watching darkness come
suns setting in unison
casting long shadows
one after another
across the years

old lost loves
you and I
clasping identical dark hands
smelling of clay and damp pine
hearing again
song of owl and loon
endless and lonesome
lingering night sounds
bouncing
echoing forever
back and forth across
a single lake
called time

Kimberly Blaeser

Where I Was That Day

It wasn't just the pill bugs
gray, many-legged and pulling that stunt
like they always did
closing in on themselves
contracting into the tiny round mass
like an image of the origin circle.
And it wasn't the turtle alone either
who became so neatly one half of the earth's sphere.

It was partly that day when I stopped at the little creek
and noticed the funny bumps on that floating log
and how they seemed to be looking at me
and how they were really little heads with beady bulging eyes
and how when I came back a half an hour later
the bumps had been rearranged on that log.

It was partly the butterflies that would materialize
out of the flower blossoms
and the deer that appeared and disappeared into the forest
while standing stock still
whose shape would be invisible one minute
and would stand out clearly the next
like an image in one of those connect-the-dot puzzles.

It was the stick bugs, the chameleon
the snakes that became branches
the opossum who was dead then suddenly alive.
And it was me who fit and saw one minute so clearly
and then stumbled blind the next
that made me think we are all always finding our place
in the great sphere of creation
that made me know I could learn a way
to pull the world around me too
to color myself with earth and air and water
and so become indistinguishable

to match my breath to the one
to pulse in and out with the mystery
to be both still and wildly alive in the same moment
to be strangely absent from myself
and yet feel large as all creation
to know
to know
to know and to belong
while the spell holds
learning to hold it a little longer each time.

That's where I was that day
I watched you from the arbor
never blinking
while you looked all about for me
and then turned back home
thinking to find me in another place
while I was there everywhere you looked.
I knew then that the stories about Geronimo were true
and that he did turn to stone
while the cavalries passed him by
mistook him for just a part of the mountain
when he had really become the whole mountain
and all the air they breathed
and even the dust beneath their horse's hooves.

I walk about trying to find the place I was that day
but getting there seems harder now
I feel heavier, my spirit weighted down
and I'm thinking I must shed something
like the animals shed their hair or skin
lose even their antlers annually
while I hold on to everything
and I'm thinking I must change my colors
like the rabbit, the ptarmigan, the weasel
and I'm thinking I must spin a cocoon
grow wings and learn to fly

and I'm thinking I must hibernate and fast
feed off my own excess for a season
and then perhaps emerge
in the place I was that day
and stay there longer this time.

And I walk about and watch the creatures
the tree toads becoming and unbecoming a part of the tree
the rocks in my path that crack open into grasshoppers and fly away
the spider who hangs suspended before me
and then disappears into mist or air
and I feel comforted
knowing we are all
in this puzzle together
knowing we are all just learning
to hold the spell
a little longer
each time.

Haiku Seasons

I. Autumn

Hoof prints in soft clay
hollowed by fine deer potter
still holding night rain.

Downy woodpecker
sidles up shag bark hickory
tat-tatting for food.

Geese black silhouettes
tangled tracery of trees
sketch fall gothic skies.

II. Winter

Pine weighted with snow
one branch launches white burden
springs up down, waving.

Juncos line the branch
slash marks on the calendar
counting days till spring.

Yesterday's snowman
how soon folds weeping to earth
gravity of warmth.

Kimberly Blaeser

III. Spring

Four fluffed doves
plump line on snowy branch
tin drip of spring thaw.

Language of droplets
ping ponging gutter downspouts
overheard spring nights.

On May's brown plowed earth
only swaying black neck stems
honking into dusk.

IV. Summer

Thumbnail size tree frogs
rise, scatter like popping corn
fill my morning walk.

Birch limbs over lake
leaves shimmer reflected light
turn green silver green.

Fat pile of puppies
tangled in afternoon sun
sleep until hungry.

V. Infinity

Many times I glimpse
feeding bird or clump of earth
one returns my look.

Recite the Names of All the Suicided Indians

I
Do it under your breath he said,
this guy back home.
Telling me something
about chanting.
Until the little bones
behind each ear
pound.
And the air swirls
off the sides
of your tongue.
Until the words
become
small projectiles.
Huffed out
of your chest
alive.

II
His uncle's boy
handcuffed
roughed up.
Hard set chin
quivering
beneath cakes of blood.
His little sister
crooked braid
falling down her back
falling down
hung over
from her first big drunk.
Those times
he stood by.
Without the words.

Kimberly Blaeser

III
Whittling matchsticks
drumming
humming with his fingertips.
Lighting smoking-wicked lamps
that smell like stories.
Shuffling decks of cards
and playing them out
hand
after aging
hand
Betting on memories
we gather here
in his house,
Until someone's ghost
begins to sing
and this year
finally
we learn to join in.

IV
Obituaries
read like tribal rolls
he says,
and saves his rice money.
Memorial wreathes
cost more each year.
Too many die
from lack of the language.
Too many too young
too Indian or too little.

Gashkendam.
He is lonesome.
So many gone silent
like the songs.
Go deaf if you must he said
but keep singing your name
your life
keep singing
your name
your life.
Nagamon.
Sing.

V
So let me
chant
for you
each one
The names
of all
the suicided
Indians.

Kimberly Blaeser

Rewriting Your Life

not just the part
that matters the most,

but those haunting scenes
that make anger and panic rise in your throat
at the domestic quarrels of strangers.
The same sort
that make my pulse pound in my ears
to drown out that saccharine alcohol voice
of the woman two booths away.

Erasing, replacing
the longings that arose from want
the causes
of your jacket fetish
the causes
of the bathtub in my parent's yard
the causes
of all old patterns stumbling on to renew themselves
of personal quirks
and other small tortures.

The children we were
we are.

I've added
a child with chink eyes
to those
bruised souls
whose lives
I rewrite
on my bluest days
and in the midst of my happiest moments
some part that seems physical
surges
with a longing
to repair
the past.

The aches in our bones are memories I'm told.
The tearing and stitching of our flesh
not the physical wear of age
really small but impossible hopes
dreamed endlessly
in smoke-filled pool halls
in one-room cold-water flats
dreams of grease-splattered arms
taking shorthand
legs crossed at the ankles
just above a pair of black patent leather pumps.

The little tug in our voices
we wash down with complimentary water
at public podiums and in banquet halls
it is the pull of the small store of joy
of a people born poor
studying in school to be ashamed
it is the shiny marbles
our children shot across muddy school yards
and then washed and lined neatly to dry
it is fresh winter snow served with cream and sugar
nickel tent movies
and hurrah for the fourth of july!

It is your memories too now
that raise the flesh on my arms and legs
And perhaps in time we can write across
that other life with this one,
never enough to obscure it
just enough to make a new pattern
a new design
pitifully inadequate perhaps
for all that has happened—
but beautiful as only loved pain can be.

Kimberly Blaeser

And so I write across your life that way
with mine
I write across your life with love
that comes from my own pain
and then, of course,
I write your face across my pain.

Apprenticed to Justice

The weight of ashes
from burned out camps.
Lodges smoulder in fire,
animal hides wither
their mythic images shrinking
pulling in on themselves,
all incinerated
fragments
of breath bone and basket
rest heavy
sink deep
like wintering frogs.
And no dustbowl wind
can lift
this history
of loss.

Now fertilized by generations—
ashes upon ashes,
this old earth erupts.
Medicine voices rise like mists
white buffalo memories
teeth marks on birch bark
forgotten forms
tremble into wholeness.

And the grey weathered stumps,
trees and treaties
cut down
trampled for wealth.
Flat Potlatch plateaus
of ghost forests
raked by bears
soften rot inward
until tiny arrows of green

Kimberly Blaeser

sprout
rise erect
rootfed
from each crumbling center.

Some will never laugh
as easily.
Will hide knives
silver as fish in their boots,
hoard names
as if they could be stolen
as easily as land,
will paper their walls
with maps and broken promises,
scar their flesh
with this badge
heavy as ashes.

And this is a poem
for those
apprenticed
from birth.
In the womb
of your mother nation
heartbeats
sound like drums
drums like thunder
thunder like twelve thousand
walking
then ten thousand
then eight
walking away
from stolen homes
from burned out camps
from relatives fallen
as they walked
then crawled
then fell.

This is the woodpecker sound
of an old retreat.
It becomes an echo.
an accounting
to be reconciled.
This is the sound
of trees falling in the woods
when they are heard,
of red nations falling
when they are remembered.
This is the sound
we hear
when fist meets flesh
when bullets pop against chests
when memories rattle hollow in stomachs.
And we turn this sound
over and over again
until it becomes
fertile ground
from which we will build
new nations
upon the ashes of our ancestors.
Until it becomes
the rattle of a new revolution
these fingers
drumming on keys.

Shirley Brozzo

Circle of Life

Some day I will make my circle of life
necklace. I will start with

one red bead	for the redman who is my ancestor; my sisters and brothers who have struggled against assimilation to survive.
one black bead	for my people of dark skin who have fought back from slavery and oppression.
one pink bead	for all my kin who share both red and white blood and find it hard to live "on the fence."
one brown bead	for all my family who share black and light blood and also walk the wire.
one blue bead	for the sky and water.
one yellow bead	for my relatives in the Orient.
one white bead	for my white family, who don't always have it so hard . . . and for those who do.
one purple bead	for my sisters who love each other.
one multicolored bead	to tie them together and remind us that we are all individuals, but must live in harmony.

Someday, when I make my circle of life
necklace.

Ardie Medina Buckholtz

Blind Grandma Mary

Sitting on the splintery wooden porch,
your cotton print dress hangs loosely
on your small, brown-skinned frame.
An apron draped around your neck
And tied at the waist, as if to secure
your dress to you.

Your eyes, staring out, seeing nothing,
but you turn them inward
begin to tell us stories.
Your voice carries us back
while your fingers search
move over the blackberries in the pan.
You lift them to your lips, rolling them
around in your toothless mouth,
savoring the sweet juice.

I do not remember your stories,
left them behind in my rush to see
the world outside our reservation.
Now I search the ghosts of my memory
seeking the words you spoke.

We did not hear of your passing
in time to help send you off
on your final journey,
across the river to where our
relations dwell, waiting in welcome.
They say you were carried out the back
window to trick bad spirits who might wait
for you at the front door.
For this I am glad.

Ardie Medina Buckholtz

Now as I sit with memories
I become a young girl again
remembering those hot summer days
spent on your front porch.
I go there from time to time
to visit with you again.

Snapshot

Propped against the wall
at the back of the table,
it rests forlornly.
Encased in a slim
wooden frame
smooth with wear,
it looks out into the room.
Fingerprints on the glass
measure its years of
lying in state, layers of
emotions from loving hands.

And so there they sit,
after all these years,
separated physically by
the chairs they occupied
for one moment, captured
forever in a picture that belies
their lifetime of togetherness.

She sits lightly on the edge
of the chair, ankles crossed,
body bent slightly forward,
ready, leaning into action.
Her dark dress accentuates
the paleness of her hand,
resting palm-down in her lap.
The raised veins trace paths across
the back of her hand, visible
proof of a life spent in labor.
Her head turned slightly
toward him, her eyes fixed
on his face, a smile graces
her lips and somehow you
know it is a smile reserved
for him alone.

Ardie Medina Buckholtz

He rests easy in the chair,
his whole body taking in the
form and function of it, using
it for all it's worth.
His shirt soiled around the neck
his pants faded at the knee
evidence of a day that is
crowded with work, where
a man rises before the sun
beds down long after its setting.
His left hand grips his knee,
fingers long, knuckles misshapen,
nails dark with the mark of his toil.
He is smiling into the camera
face etched with the lines of a
wind and sunburned existence.
His eyes sharp and bright
crinkle at the corners, his gaze
steady and sure.

But it is not the separateness of
their bodies that draws attention.
There is more, a thousand words spoken
in their hands—his right, her left
resting on the arms of their chairs
so close,
almost touching
but not quite.
Years of a side-by-side
togetherness
the strength of union that goes
beyond the simpleness of
everyday living.

And now they reside, on the
back of the table, as their loved
ones carry on with their lives,
occasionally glancing at the
picture, every so often picking it
up to look closely at the image
of a man and woman
held captive in a worn frame,
sensing more than just that image.

And never has it occurred to
the family to replace the
frame for to do so
would alter the history
of a man beside his wife.

Ardie Medina Buckholtz

The Weaver

I am a weaver
have lived my life
strung out
like so many threads.
Not tethered to any loom,
I blow in scattered symmetry.
At your leaving
the threads dangle
I pull together
tangled lines of hurt.
One by one
I separate them
their colors brilliant with feelings:
   my black anger   from purple grief
   yellow disbelief beige loneliness.
Pulling the past out of these
lifeless links,
I begin again
this familiar task of
weaving my life back together.
I plait pain with pleasure,
knot love with longing
loop solitude with need.
The pattern never changes.
I weave, it unravels.
I love, it unravels.
You walk away with
one of my life threads
tied to your heart.
I am unraveling
and no one
but the weaver
in me
is left to see.

Returning

The single lane dirt road alternates
small rocks, smooth sand. Her bare feet
skim the small rocks
she scuffs the smooth, cool sand through her toes.

Tall pine trees hover, familiar and comfortable
companions, their branches offering her shade
from the hot sun. Ripe, juicy
blackberries wash the dust from her throat.

She rounds the bend. The house looms
before her, its peeling paint like bark
from a white birch. A black car greets her
from the front yard, weeds snaking through its rusted shell.

Blackie's white-whiskered eyes register her
approach with a slow, disinterested blink. His tail
wags faintly, waving her on, dismissing her.

Pauline Danforth

They Went to Douglas Lodge

A child sits by an old woman
a bundle of sweet grass between them
my mother explains, the child is herself
the old woman, her grandmother
together they weave sweet grass baskets
sweet smelling, fragrant from the rain

her mother a young widow sits nearby
dreaming under prairie skies
as she bends dry, curled birch bark
into miniature canoes and baskets

Aunt Jane carefully stitches a puckered top
mocassins for a baby she will never hold
Aunt Mary beads swirling red roses
onto black velvet cut for a tiny purse

Old and blind great-grandma
braids bright rag rugs from remnant calico
the children help her find the colors
one knot for yellow, two knots for blue

Young daughters, old women together they work
old ones teaching young ones, gently guiding
little hands, teaching them the old ways
fashioned for the new

Clear, crisp morning, breakfast at daybreak
fire smoke spirals upward signaling a busy day
Grandpa hitches the horses, stomping and snorting
carefully packing beadwork, baskets, moccasins and rugs
for the twenty mile trip through the pine forest

The children play quietly, waiting
listening at dusk for the jingle of horse harness
their mouths watering, knowing that candy
is hidden just for them in Grandpa's pocket

Pauline Danforth

Basel, Switzerland

Crooked, cobbled streets all lead to the Rhine River
Staunch row houses stand in rigid formality
Turrets, spires and chimneys reach for the sky
Just as the complacent scarlet begonias do
All seeking the reclusive autumn sun

Old Basel, crossroads of cultures
Traders from the east bring silk and spices
From the south, one hundred varieties of cheeses
And from the north, fine wine to whet one's palate
For stout German stews, French pastries, Swiss candies
Street cafes edge Basel's narrow streets
Their competing aromas enticing passersby

Emil, he sees it all, the parade of Baselers,
Young mothers, matrons, students and bankers
At Markplatz they mingle with tourists
Whose blood forgets but cries to remember
Ancestral graves on the Rhine and in the rising Alps
They strut in their L.L. Bean finery like curious peacocks
Looking with eager curiosity, perhaps like the visiting kings
Who met at the Drei Konige so many centuries ago

Modern students, descendants of Heidegger and Hegel
Sip their coffee, that elixir of contemplation
Vehemently arguing being and existence
Ink-stained fingers thumbing their scholars texts
And there's the busy Swiss banker,
Briefcase in hand, he is the only one at Markplatz
The vagaries of world economics rule his beleaguered path

Emil, with his faded beret and droopy mustache
He just sells his produce, he doesn't care what tongue you speak
Gestures say it all in this town of Babel
Oh, the seasons change and his bins brim
First with strawberries, then apples and autumn squash
Emil, he chews his licorice and watches it all
At Markplatz, at Basel, crossroads of Europe

Pauline Danforth

The vanishing whiteman

I spent my childhood chasing my father's shadow
Down dark alleys and around street corners
He was elusive, impossible to catch
I wanted to pounce on him and stomp him dead
But he vanished into thin air

Like generations of white men before him
He got the Indian girl, but married his own kind
I grew up Indian and proud, my white blood was my shame
Now a stranger lurks within me
When I look in the mirror, he is gone

For my schizophrenic sister

Little sister, your belly round with male child
It seems like yesterday we made mud pies together
Remember when you were four, you followed me to school?
Lost and afraid, you walked the school halls calling my name
I left my fourth grade classroom and dried your tears
You let me hold your hand as we crossed the busy street
Little sister, it's been a long time since you let me care for you

You grew tall and became a rebel, sassing back and staying out late
Without emotion, you bent over for the belt on your donkey
This word from your imaginative childhood language
Then you ran away, living on the street and in foster homes
Sitting in our bedroom, one twin bed empty, I willed you to return
Little sister, do you know how sad I was to lose you?

Remember, you wanted to be a psychologist back then?
You who hears voices whispering obscenities and cursing your name
From your tidy high rise efficiency, you tell me of intruders
Who muddle your cupboards, rearranging your canisters
You defy textbook labels, making me promise to not say the "S" word
Little sister, do you know I love you just as you are?

Inside your woman shell, your gentle child spirit still lives
We visit the Rose Garden where the child spirit gathers velvet petals
With your watercolors, you studiously dab flowers in pastel brilliance
Leaning back you outline puffy lions in the cotton candy clouds
Later driving by elegant mansions we choose our future homes

Pauline Danforth

Little sister, food shelf patron and regular diner at the House of Charity
Your meager disability check is spent on cable TV you don't watch
I bring you groceries and you pay me back on the first of the month
Defending your independence, my generosity becomes a loan
Can't you see that accepting my help would be a gift to me?

Your life is like a jigsaw puzzle, connected but in pieces
You think your baby will make it complete and connect you to life
Instead you are only adding a piece to your puzzle
Little sister, somehow you have survived, somehow you will survive

Pauline Danforth

Star Husband

His drinking drove her there
to that open place in the woods
where at dusk the deer come to feed
in the circle of trees

On hot summer days she walked barefoot
up the hill to hear the crickets sing
and watch garter snakes
slither through the waist-high grass
seeking the warmth of the boulders
near the rocky path leading down to the house

That still night when the stars were so close
you could almost touch them, she found
solace in the quiet comfort of the circling trees

On the largest boulder, cool in the night air
she sat and gazed longingly upon one bright star
wishing herself up to the sky
In a twinkling of light from a falling star
he came for her, her star husband
we haven't seen her since
though at night we see two stars lingering low
over that circle of trees.

Pauline Danforth

On the birth of my nephew

Little drummer boy, your heartbeat thumps quiet and steady
Through the night in this siren city that never sleeps
The pulsating rhythm captured on the monitor tells us you are safe
Languishing sleepily in your amniotic bed
While in this shadowed room your mother and I await your birth

Little drummer boy, so serene in your protective belly shell
Do you hear the ambulances wailing in the night?
Carrying damaged bodies to the midnight fluorescence below
Wrecked by life, they moan in pain, their souls wounded

Little drummer boy, unaware of peril, your future is an unwritten book
You don't know the dangers lurking in these city streets
Here in the hospital room, your heartbeat lulls me to a ragged sleep
I dream of you pausing at life's door, while others beg to stay

Anne Dunn

Their Eyes
Inspired by a Lewis Hines photo

Their eyes have followed me home
Across a span of 90 years.
Round-shouldered,
Narrow-chested,
Sooty-faced
Children laboring
In darknesses
Concealed from
Square-shouldered,
Full-chested,
Rosy-faced
Children warming
In well-lit parlors.

Coal mine urchins
Sick on dust by 12,
Bent forever
Over endless chutes.
Catching the stones
That do not burn.
Beaten for looking up.

"Reach too far and, Boy,
You've had it!"
Mangled, torn and broken.
Or carried down the chute
To smother in the coal.
Worth pennies as they toil.
Worth nothing as they die.
Their eyes have followed me home.

Anne Dunn

Tangerine Light

In the tangerine light of dusk
Children play.

Laughing little ones,
Their small feet kicking dust.

Climbing into a burned out bus
They take turns driving
To a far safe place
Somewhere beyond
Nasiriyah, Iraq

Mother's Garden

I remember how the squash
Climbed the wire fence
In Mother's summer garden,
Their sprawling arms moving quickly
Toward the sun, clutching tiny fruit
In small green gloves.
At last they reached the top
And tumbled over with open hands
Revealing sacred golden orbs.
They scurried to the shelter
Of a robust tomato nation
Where they lay nurtured and secure.
Toads spoke to them of forgotten ones,
Children who read in garden leaves
Secrets of corn and mysteries of beans.
The plump squash grew rich and ripe
As I sat alone in Mother's garden
Reading leaves of corn and beans.

Anne Dunn

Let Me Tell You

Fox came to our sweat
On a frosty night.
She entered the first door,
Stepped quickly inside,
Shook her tail and shivered.
Then she sat at my right.
Blinking her bright eyes,
She barked, "Can't start without me!
You shouldn't even try."
Soon the door was closed.
She choked on the intense heat.
With her small dark paw pressed
Against my arm, she gasped.
I hung my wet towel over her.

At the second door Wolf came
Stepping 'round the silent circle.
He sat at my left,
Raised his head and howled.
"Let me tell you how
The moon rose from the river
While fog spirits danced
On muskrat's scattered lodges.
Let me tell you how
The rain fell softly
Over my mate
Suffering in a metal snare
Laid by bloody men
Who kill our nation wantonly."
He leaned against my shoulder,
Touching my face
With his warm tongue.

Bear arrived at the third door,
Circled the lodge seven times,
Smelling each of us within.
Speaking through the wall
He said, "Beware those
Deceiving spirits of confusion.
Beware their grace and charm."

I heard Bear walking north
As Heron came from the south.
Standing on the sweat lodge
She transformed to Woman,
Tore a hole in the roof, reached in
And pierced me with a long, cold finger.
Afterwards we gathered at the altar,
Covered our heads with ash and wept
For our helpers and our friends.

Anne Dunn

Doctor Zhivago

He returned to Lara ice-encrusted.
Held upright by the frost in his coat.

All that night I clung to warmth.
Fearful that a frozen man
Would stumble to my door,
Begging for my blanket

Heid Erdrich

True Myth

Tell a child she is composed of parts
(her Ojibway quarters, her German half-heart)
she'll find the existence of harpies easy
to swallow. Storybook children never come close
to her mix, but manticores make great uncles.
Sphinx a cousin she'll allow, centaurs better to love
than boys—the horse part, at least, she can ride.
With a bestiary for a family album she's proud.
Her heap of blankets, her garbage grin, prove
she's descended of bears, her totem, it's true.
And that German witch with the candy roof,
that was her ancestor too. If swans can rain
white rape from heaven, then what is a girl to do?
Believe her Indian eyes, her sly French smile,
her breast with its veins of skim milk blue—
She is the myth that is true.

Heid Erdrich

Poem for Our Ojibwe Names

Those stars shine words right
into the center of the dream:

Gego zegizi kane.
Gego zegizi kane.
Maajii'am.
Maajii nii'm.
Majii gigidoon.

So it is when we have our names:

We will not fear.
We start to sing,
to dance, to speak.

When we did not know him
the stick man, the running man,
came jigging in our dreams.
Always in motion like a wooden toy,
he sang *"Bakenatay, Bakenatay"*
so deeply his voice was a root.

So too the woman wrapped in red wool,
whose laughter woke us, *"ChiWaabeno."*
She spoke the word for dreamers—
then teased in diminishment, *"Waaban-ish."*
Still her meaning took us years to learn.

Gego zegizi kane.
Gego zegizi kane.
Maajii'am
Maajii nii'm
Majii gigidoon

So it is when we have our names:
We will not fear.
We start to sing,
to dance, to speak.

It is not what you imagine,
no matter what you imagine.
Stars shine stories.
Words come speaking into our dreams.

Heid Erdrich

Memorial

I do not walk among ruins as tourists do.
My travels to far cities never agenda
strolls among the tombs, except one
visit to the sphinx-headed monument,
Morrison's grave, strewn with offerings:
wine bottles and needles. I do not walk
bow-headed in honor of the dead. I always
thought I'd want to be buried in the sky—
my Plains ancestors' way: stashed in the fork
of a great cottonwood with rushing leaves.
Until this clear morning after storm,
when we wake to power, water, phone
all gone. We emerge as dazed as squirrels
who approach us, passive, damp, blinking,
as if we could explain this inverted world—
huge trees down, their massive roots won't loose
their grip on water pipes, gas lines, electric cables,
our human roots hauled up, exposed.
All day we view the trees as they lie in state,
fallen leaders, enormous memorials to their own demise.
The size of the trees! Their huge souls—like whales
or elephants heaped upon our road. The crews saw
through to pavement. Finally the street's revealed,
newly lit and bright as any eternal flame.
The trees' remains stagger down the block like stones,
rows of memorials, a stump yard for the greats.
We bow our heads and move towards shade.

Nesting Dolls

I've been golden in the long afterglow,
I've been that bubble in the honey pot,
I've been sweet, sweet in me
and all along someone else.
That's the mystery.
First the man gives up his driblet of will,
it leaves his body to enter mine and in a moment
start another body that will leave mine.
It's what we all crave and sense; the memory
of such harmony, then a series of losses, separations.
The egg, the gold bubble in me, once in my Ojibwe mother,
once in her Ojibwe mother, and so on back
like nesting dolls. Now we tip the jar,
watch the slow pour of gold, the bubble thins
grows toward self, toward that lovely love of self.

Heid Erdrich

Vermillion Hands Petroglyph

Red ochre on rock, this kiss you blew
in pigment that outlines your hand.
Centuries waved by, gesture sealed
with the lasting bond the sturgeon
taught us—her leaping look,
the bend of her linked spine,
saurian, ancient, enduring.

Teach me back into time
Until I know there is no time.
My hand in yours for years and years.

Heid Erdrich

Mindimoyeg: Dandelions

I thought, why cut them out?
A weed so cheery on the boulevard,
first thing to bloom in Spring—
But the retired Emperor of the Neighborhood,
crossed the street, shoved a dandelion fork
in my hand, asked did I know what it was
demanded I use it.

Who can blame him?
His whole generation groomed lawns
next-to-godly clean. Chemicals
and edger rentals: The American Dream.
My weeds might invade, take each lawn,
year by year, until all this Spring cheer would
nod up and down the avenue.

That would not do. Not a fair fight,
since this species long ago arrived, took over,
became so valued by the people here
that they named it for their elders:
Mindimoya, Old Woman, Ojibwe call them.
White-headed in a day, yet full of seedy
vigor—most fertile once they've aged.

When young, the mindimoya helps
new mothers get their milk: notched leaves bleed
white sap, a bitter tonic that perhaps works
as a suggestive cure. Or is there science here?
So many of the old medicines have come to signify.

Heid Erdrich

I might have tried it, had I been desperate to get
a baby on my breast. Nothing could taste worse
than hungry infant cries. But no, my son slept sated
in a basket nearby where I dug the milky roots,
all the while apologizing to the strong old ones,
asking that they give up their hold on the place.

And though I piled them high, blistered my hand
where the fork fit, next year they returned.
Our young neighbors made a pact to just let them go.
And the old ladies nod now, Empresses of the Avenue.

"Mindimoyeg: Dandelions" uses one of the Ojibwe names for dandelions
that means old women. Another name, *dodo-jibik,* refers to milk.

Offering: First Rice

For Jim Northrup

The grains should be green as river rocks,
long as hayseed, with the scent of duckweed
and sweetgrass that grows along the lake's banks.
First *manoomin*, feast plate laid for the spirits—
berries and tobacco offered with song.
What it must have meant to give
what little the people had to give:
herbs left in thanks for the food that will sustain us,
for the water that gives up that food,
for the world working the way it should
—living and full of living god.

Heid Erdrich

Offering: Ojibwe

Some leaf taps the classroom window.
I am wondering what's the Ojibwe word for poem,
while my teacher says, *There is a spirit*
who helps the language live.
We should make offerings to that alive
spirit and ask for help.
Then he gives the quiz.
I bomb it because the words leap live
from the page to the open window
where the spirit catches them, quizzes:
Was it the one who was trying to write a poem?
Tell her to open the window and drift an offering down.

Sometime before the end of this poem
I go outside, try to ask that spirit,
who's got its job cut out, for help.
I think: *I do not have the right, the right words.*
And back beside my window: *I only have my poems.*
Then words drift, offering in their own right their own life.

Louise Erdrich

Indian Boarding School: The Runaways

Home's the place we head for in our sleep.
Boxcars stumbling north in dreams
don't wait for us. We catch them on the run.
The rails, old lacerations that we love,
shoot parallel across the face and break
just under Turtle Mountains. Riding scars
you can't get lost. Home is the place they cross.

The lame guard strikes a match and makes the dark
less tolerant. We watch through cracks in boards
as the land starts rolling, rolling till it hurts
to be here, cold in regulation clothes.
We know the sheriff's waiting at midrun
to take us back. His car is dumb and warm.
The highway doesn't rock, it only hums
like a wing of long insults. The worn-down welts
of ancient punishments lead back and forth.

All runaways wear dresses, long green ones,
the color you would think shame was. We scrub
the sidewalks down because it's shameful work.
Our brushes cut the stone in watered arcs
and in the soak frail outlines shiver clear
a moment, things us kids pressed on the dark
face before it hardened, pale, remembering
delicate old injuries, the spines of names and leaves.

Louise Erdrich

Turtle Mountain Reservation

For Pat Gourneau, my grandfather

The heron makes a cross
flying low over the marsh.
Its heart is an old compass
pointing off in four directions.
It drags the world along,
the world it becomes.

My face surfaces in the green
beveled glass above the washstand.
My handprint in thick black powder
on the bedroom shade.
Home I could drink like thin fire
that gathers
like lead in my veins,
heart's armor, the coffee stains.

In the dust of the double hollyhock,
Theresa, one frail flame eating wind.
One slim candle
that snaps in the dry grass.
Ascending tall ladders
that walk to the edge of dusk.
Riding a blue cricket
through the tumult of the falling dawn.

At dusk the gray owl walks the length of the roof,
sharpening its talons on the shingles.
Grandpa leans back
between spoonfuls of canned soup
and repeats to himself a word
that belongs to a world
no one else can remember.

The day has not come
when from sloughs, the great salamander
lumbers through snow, salt, and fire
to be with him, throws the hatchet
of its head through the door of the three-room house
and eats the blue roses that are peeling off the walls.

Uncle Ray, drunk for three days
behind the jagged window
of a new government box,
drapes himself in fallen curtains, and dreams that the odd
beast seen near Cannonball, North Dakota,
crouches moaning at the door to his body. The latch
is the small hook and eye

of religion. Twenty nuns
fall through clouds to park their butts
on the metal hasp. Surely that
would be considered miraculous almost anyplace,

but here in the Turtle Mountains
it is no more than common fact.
Raymond wakes,
but he can't shrug them off. He is looking up
dark tunnels of their sleeves,
and into their frozen armpits,
or is it heaven? He counts the points
of their hairs like stars.

One by one they blink out,
and Theresa comes forth
clothed in the lovely hair
she has been washing all day. She smells
like a hayfield, drifting pollen
of birch trees.
Her hair steals across her shoulders
like a postcard sunset.

Louise Erdrich

All the boys tonight, goaded from below,
will approach her in The Blazer, The Tomahawk,
The White Roach Bar where everyone
gets up to cut the rug, wagging everything they got,
as the one bass drum of The Holy Greaseballs
lights a depth
charge through the smoke.

Grandpa leans closer to the bingo.
The small fortune his heart pumps for
is hidden in the stained, dancing numbers.
The Ping-Pong balls rise through colored lights,
brief as sparrows
God is in the sleight of the woman's hand.

He walks from Saint Ann's, limp and crazy
as the loon that calls its children
across the lake
in its broke, knowing laughter.
Hitchhiking home from the Mission, if he sings,
it is a loud, rasping wail
that saws through the spine
of Ira Comes Last, at the wheel.

Drawn up through the neck ropes,
drawn out of his stomach
by the spirit of the stones that line
the road and speak
to him only in their old agreement.
Ira knows the old man is nuts.
Lets him out at the road that leads up
over stars and the skulls of white cranes.

And through the soft explosions of cattail
and the scattering of seeds on still water,
walks Grandpa, all the time that there is in his hands
that have grown to be the twisted doubles
of the burrows of mole and badger,
that have come to be the absence
of birds in a nest.
Hands of earth, of this clay
I'm also made from.

Louise Erdrich

Spring Evening on Blind Mountain

I won't drink wine tonight
I want to hear what is going on
not in my own head
but all around me.
I sit for hours
outside our house on Blind Mountain.
Below this scrap of yard
across the ragged old pasture,
two horses move
pulling grass into their mouths, tearing up
wildflowers by the roots.
They graze shoulder to shoulder.
Every night they lean together in sleep.
Up here, there is no one
for me to fail.
You are gone.
Our children are sleeping.
I don't even have to write this down.

Captivity

He (my captor) gave me a bisquit, which I put in my pocket, and not daring to eat it,
buried it under a log, fearing he had put something in it that make me love him.—
from the narrative of the captivity of Mrs. Mary Rowlandson, who was taken
prisoner by the Wampanoag when Lancaster, Massachusetts, was destroyed, in
the year 1676

The stream was swift, and so cold
I thought I would be sliced in two.
But he dragged me from the flood
by the ends of my hair.
I had grown to recognize his face.
I could distinguish it from the others.
There were times I feared I understood
his language, which was not human,
and I knelt to pray for strength.

We were pursued! By God's agents
or pitch devils I did not know.
Only that we must march.
Their guns were loaded with swan shot.
I could not suckle and my child's wail
put them in danger.
He had a woman
with teeth black and glittering.
She fed the child milk of acorns.
The forest closed, the light deepened.

I told myself that I would starve
before I took food from his hands
but I did not starve.
One night
he killed a deer with a young one in her
and gave me to eat of the fawn.
It was so tender,
the bones like the stems of flowers,
that I followed where he took me.

Louise Erdrich

The night was thick. He cut the cord
that bound me to the tree.

After that the birds mocked.
Shadows gaped and roared
and the trees flung down
their sharpened lashes.
He did not notice God's wrath.
God blasted fire from half-buried stumps.
I hid my face in my dress, fearing He would burn us all
but this, too, passed.

Rescued, I see no truth in things.
My husband drives a thick wedge
through the earth, still it shuts
to him year after year.
My child is fed of the first wheat.
I lay myself to sleep
on a Holland-laced pillowbeer.
I lay to sleep.
And in the dark I see myself
as I was outside their circle.

They knelt on deerskins, some with sticks,
and he led his company in the noise
until I could no longer bear
the thought of how I was.
I stripped a branch
and struck the earth,
in time, begging it to open
to admit me
as he was
and feed me honey from the rock.

Shelter

My four adopted sons in photographs
wear solemn black. Their faces comprehend
their mother's death, an absence in a well
of empty noise, and Otto strange and lost.
Her name was Mary also, Mary Kröger.
Two of us have lived and one is gone.
Her hair was blond; it floated back in wings,
and still you see her traces in the boys:
bright hair and long, thin, knotted woman's hands.
I knew her, Mary Kröger, and we were bosom friends.
All graves are shelters for our mislaid twins.

Otto was for many years her husband,
and that's the way I always thought of him.
I nursed her when she sickened and the cure
fell through at Rochester. The healing bath
that dropped her temperature, I think, too fast.
I was in attendance at her death:
She sent the others out. She rose and gripped my arm
and tried to make me promise that I'd care
for Otto and the boys. I had to turn away
as my own mother had when her time came.
How few do not return in memory
and make us act in ways we can't explain.
I could not lie to ease her, living, dying.
All graves are full of such accumulation.
And yet, the boys were waiting in New York
to take the first boat back to Otto's folks
in Germany, prewar, dark powers were at work,
and Otto asked me on the westbound bus
to marry him. I could not tell him no—
We help our neighbors out. I loved him though.

Louise Erdrich

It took me several years to know I did
from that first time he walked in to deliver
winter food. Through Father Adler's kitchen,
he shouldered half an ox like it was bread
and looked at me too long for simple greeting.
This is how our lives complete themselves,
as effortless as weather, circles blaze
in ordinary days, and through our waking selves
they reach, to touch our true and sleeping speech.

So I took up with Otto, took the boys
and watched for them, and made their daily bread
from what the grocer gave them in exchange
for helping him. It's hard to tell you how
they soon became so precious I got sick
from worry, and woke up for two months straight
and had to check them, sleeping, in their beds
and had to watch and see each breathe or move
before I could regain my sleep again.
All graves are pregnant with our nearest kin.

The Red Sleep of Beasts

On space of about an acre I counted two hundred and twenty of these
animals; the banks of the river were covered thus with these animals as far
as the eye could reach and in all directions. One may judge now, if it is
possible, the richness of these prairies.
　　　　　　　　　　　　　—from a letter by Father Belcourt,
a missionary who accompanied the Michif on one of their last buffalo
hunts in the 1840s;
　　　　　　　North Dakota Historical Collections, Volume V

We heard them when they left the hills,
Low hills where they used to winter and bear their young.
Blue hills of oak and birch that broke the wind.
They swung their heavy muzzles, wet with steam,
And broke their beards of breath to breathe.

We used to hunt them in our red-wheeled carts.
Frenchmen gone *sauvage,* how the women burned
In scarlet sashes, black wool skirts.
For miles you heard the ungreased wood
Groan as the load turned.

Thunder was the last good hunt.
Great bales of skins and meat in iron cauldrons
Boiling through the night. We made our feast
All night, but still we could not rest.

We lived headlong, taking what we could
But left no scraps behind, not like the other
Hide hunters, hidden on a rise,
Their long-eyes brought herds one by one
To earth. They took but tongues, and you could walk
For miles across the strange hulks.

Louise Erdrich

We wintered in the hills. Low huts of log
And trampled dirt, the spaces tamped with mud.
At night we touched each other in our dreams
Hearing, on the wind, their slow hooves stumbling

South, we said at first, the old ones knew
They would not come again to the low hills.
We heard them traveling, heard the frozen birches
Break before their long retreat
Into the red sleep.

The Sacraments

Baptism, Communion, Confirmation,
Matrimony, Holy Orders, Extreme Unction

1

As the sun dancers, in their helmets of sage,
stopped at the sun's apogee
and stood in the waterless light,
so, after loss, it came to this:
that for each year the being was destroyed,
I was to sacrifice a piece of my flesh.
The keen knife hovered
and the skin flicked in the bowl.
Then the sun, the life that consumes us,
burst into agony.

We began, the wands and the bracelets of sage,
the feathers cocked over our ears.
When the bird joined the circle and called,
we cried back, shrill breath,
through the bones in our teeth.
Her wings closed over us, her dark red
claws drew us upward by the scars,
so that we hung by the flesh,

as in the moment before birth
when the spirit is quenched
in whole pain, suspended
until there is no choice, the body
slams to earth,
the new life starts.

Louise Erdrich

2

It is spring. The tiny frogs pull
their strange new bodies out
of the suckholes, the sediment of rust,
and float upward, each in a silver bubble
that breaks on the water's surface,
to one clear unceasing note of need.

Sometimes, when I hear them,
I leave our bed and stumble
among the white shafts of weeds
to the edge of the pond.
I sink to the throat,
and witness the ravenous trill
of the body transformed at last and then consumed
in a rush of music.

Sing to me, sing to me.
I have never been so cold
rising out of sleep.

3

I was twelve, in my body
three eggs were already marked
for the future.
Two golden, one dark.
And the man,
he was selected from other men,
by a blow on the cheek
similar to mine.
That is how we knew,
from the first meeting.
There was no question
There was the wound.

4

It was frightening, the trees in their rigid postures
using up the sun,
as the earth tilted its essential degree.
Snow covered everything. Its confusing glare
doubled the view
so that I saw you approach
my empty house
not as one man, but as a landscape
repeating along the walls of every room
papering over the cracked grief.
I knew as I stepped into the design,
as I joined the chain of hands,
and let the steeple of fire
be raised above our heads.
We had chosen the costliest pattern,
the strangest, the most enduring.
We were afraid as we stood between the willows,
as we shaped the standard words with our tongues.
Then it was done. The scenery multiplied
around us and we turned.
We stared calmly from the pictures.

5

God, I was not meant to be the isolate
cry in this body.
I was meant to have your tongue in my mouth.

That is why I stand by your great plaster lips
waiting for your voice to unfold from its dark slot.

Your hand clenched in the shape of a bottle.
Your mouth painted shut on the answer.
Your eyes, two blue mirrors, in which I am perfectly denied.

I open my mouth and I speak
though it is only a thin sound, a leaf
scraping on a leaf.

Louise Erdrich

6

When the blue steam stalls over the land
and the resinous apples
turn to mash, then to a cider whose thin
twang shrivels the tongue,
the snakes hatch
twirling from the egg.
In the shattered teacup, from the silvering
boards of the barn,
in the heat of rotting mulch hay,
they soak up the particles of light

so that all winter
welded in the iron sheath
of sludge under the pond
they continue, as we do,
drawing closer to the source,
their hearts beating slower
as the days narrow
until there is this one pale aperture
and the tail sliding through

then the systole, the blackness of heaven.

Morning Fire

My baby, eating rainbows of sun
focused through a prism in my bedroom window,
puts her mouth to the transparent fire,
and licks up the candy colors
that tremble on the white sheets.
The stain spreads across her face.
She only has one tooth,
a grain of white rice
that keeps flashing.
She keeps eating as the day begins
until the rainbows are all inside of her.
And then she smiles
and such a light pours over me.
It is not that white blaze
that strikes the earth all around you
when you learn of the death
of one you love. Or the next light
that strips away your skin.
Not the radiance
that unwraps you to the bone.
Soft and original fire,
allow me to curl around you in the white sheets
and keep feeding you the light
from my own body
until we drift into the deep
of our being.
Air, fire, golden earth.

Linda LeGarde Grover

Grandmother at Indian School

Left on smooth wooden steps to think
about disobedience, and forgetfulness
she feels warm sun on the back of her neck
as she kneels on the pale spot worn
by other little girls' tender sore knees
a hundred black wool stockings
grinding skin and stairs,
beneath one knee and a hard white navy bean.

Small distant lightning flickers
pale flashes down her shins, felt by other
uniformed girls marching to sewing class
waiting for their own inevitable return
to the stair, to think and remember what happens
to girls who speak a pagan tongue.

Try to forget this pagan tongue.

Disobedient and forgetful she almost hears
beyond the schoolyard beyond
the train ride beyond
little girls crying in their small white beds

her mama far away
singing to herself as she cooks
and speaking quietly to Grandma as they sew
the quilt for mama's new baby
and laughing with her sisters
as they wash clothes

the little bean
did it hurt?

"Bizaan, gego mawi ken, don't cry"
She moves her knee so the little bean
would feel just the soft part, and not the bone
how long can I stay here?
and when Sister returns to ask if she's thought
she says yes,
I won't talk like a pagan again
and she stands and picks up the little bean
and carries it in her lonesome lying hand
until lights out
when the baby bean
sleeps under her pillow.

Linda LeGarde Grover

Saint Bernard

When I got to mission school
my worries about my mother
and how she was doing without me
had to wait when
the priest told me
I had a bigger worry than that.
When I died, he said,
they would never let me into heaven
when they heard my name.
With a name like mine *Barney*
not any kind of a Christian name at all
I couldn't float in
past the eyes of God when I died
he'd turn me away for certain
with a name like mine *Barney*

and send me back to mission school.

And so they named me after this big dog
who carried whiskey
in a little barrel around his neck
and saved people's lives
by giving them a drink.
Well, I'd heard about that
and even saw it with my own eyes
in a bar in the west end.
Thanks niji you saved my life,
a man told my uncle,
I was sure dying for a drink.
So I supposed it was all right
and tried to feel the honor
of my namesake.
But it didn't stick
and I reverted to my pagan ways.
See, when I got home
and my mother said hello Barney
I was so happy
I forgot all about heaven.

Everything You Need to Know in Life You'll Learn at Boarding School

Speak English. Forget the language of your
grandparents. It is dead. Forget their teachings.
They are unGodly and ignorant. Cleanliness is
next to Godliness. Indians are not clean. Your
parents did not teach you proper hygiene. Stay
in line. This is a toothbrush. Hang it on the hook
next to the others. Do not allow the bristles to
touch. This spreads the disease that you bring
to school from your families. Make your bed with
mitered corners. A bed not properly made will be
torn apart. Start over. Remember and be grateful
that boarding school feeds and clothes you. Say
grace before meals. In English. Don't cry. Crying
never solved anything. Write home once every
month. In English. Tell your parents that you are
doing very well. You'll never amount to anything.
Make the most of your opportunities. You'll never
amount to anything. Answer when the teacher
addresses you. In English. If your family insists on
and can provide transportation for you to visit home
in the summer, report to the matron's office immediately
upon your return. You will be allowed into the
dormitory after you have been sanitized and de-loused.
Busy hands are happy hands. Keep yourself occupied.
You'll never amount to anything. Books are our friends.
Reading is your key to the world. Forget the language
of your grandparents. It is dead. If you are heard speaking
it you will kneel on a navy bean for one hour. We will ask
if you have learned your lesson. You will answer. In English.
Spare the rod and spoil the child. We will not spare the rod.
We will cut your hair. We will shame you. We will lock you
in the basement. Learn from that. Improve yourself.
You'll never amount to anything. Speak English.

Linda LeGarde Grover

To the Woman Who Just Bought a Set of Native American Spirituality Dream Interpretation Cards

Sister, listen carefully to this.

You'll probably go right past me
when you're looking
for a real   gen-yew-whine
Indian princess
to flagellate you a little
and feed your self-indulgent
un-guilt
about what other people
not as fine-tuned and sensitive as you
did to women
by the way, women like me
who you probably go right past
when you're looking.

I know what you're looking for
and I know I'm not it.
You're looking for that other
Indian woman, you want
a for real   gen-yew-whine
oshki-traditional princess
and you'll know her when you see her
glibly glinting silver and turquoise
carrying around her own little
magic shop of real   gen-yew-whine
rattling beads and jangling charms
beaming about her moon
as she sells you a ticket to her sweat lodge.
She's a spiritual concession stand
and it's your own business to go ahead and buy
or rent it if you want to go ahead
what do I care
acquire what you will,
you've done it before.

I know what you're looking for
and I know I'm not it. Hell, no
I won't be dressing up or dancing for you
or selling you a ceremony
that women around here never heard of
I won't tell your fortune
· or interpret your dreams
so put away your money.

What you really want to buy you'll never see,
and anyway it's not for sale.

Sister, you weren't listening to this
I know, and I know too that
that authentic, guaranteed
satisfaction or your money back
gen-yew-whine for real
oshki-traditional Indian princess
is easy to find. Bring your checkbook.
Or a major credit card.
I'll be watching you both.

Linda LeGarde Grover

Nindaniss Wawashkeshikwesens on a Winter Night

In the moonlit quiet of a winter night

as I pass her bedroom door

Nindaniss Wawashkeshikwesens

my daughter the Deer Girl

springs from her bed.

While in startled graceful silence

she totters to my arms

from the distant dark forest of her sleep

her wide dark eyes ask "What? Wegonen?"

and I carefully lead her back to her bed.

"My girl, sh, sh, niban, niban,

go to sleep, go back to sleep."

Folding her long legs beneath herself

she nestles under the pile of blankets

I tuck around her

and her wide dark eyes close

as she returns to the distant dark forest sleep

of the Wawashkeshiwug.

Chi-Ko-ko-koho and the Boarding School Prefect, 1934

From my owl's nest home, unsteady greasy oak
covered by cowhide long oblivious
to claws tough and curving as old tree roots
I breathe the night breeze, starry broken glass.

I am Chi-Ko-ko-koho. My black-centered
unblinking owl eyes see past the dark
growl of this old bear den of a bar,
through stinging fog of unintended
blasphemy, tobacco's tarry prayers
stuck and dusty on a hammered tin ceiling,
to grieving spirits mirrored by my own.
I am Chi-Ko-ko-koho, young among owls
as young among lush crimson blooms of death
is the embryonic seedling in my chest,
the rooting zygote corkscrew in my chest,
these days all but unseen, a pink seaspray
sunset on the rim of a thick white coffee cup.
My grieving spirit hardly notices
though, in this old bear den of a bar.

My owl head turns clear round when I see him.

I am Chi-Ko-ko-koho, I blink away
smoke and fog, my head swivels back
and he's still there, the prefect. He's still there
and real, not some ghost back to grab my throat
again with those heavy old no-hands of his
or crack my brother's homesick skinny bones
on cold concrete tattooed by miseries
of other Indian boys who crossed his path.

To the darkness of this bear den of a bar
he's brought his own sad spirit for a drink.

Linda LeGarde Grover

I am Chi-Ko-ko-koho, but who he sees
is Kwiiwizens, a boy bent and kneeling
beneath the prefect's doubled leather strap,
and Kwiiwizens I am. My belly feels
a tiny worm the color of the moon
writhe in laughter at my cowardice
as that now embodied ghost, the old prefect
step-drags, step-drags his dampened moccasins
to my end of the bar. Sad flowers and vines
weep beaded tears in mourning for us all.

He asks me for a nickel for a beer.
With closed eyes Kwiiwizens waits for the strap.

Chi-Ko-ko-koho dives from his grimy perch
to yank the apparition by the hair,
then flies him past the blind face of the moon
to drop him in the alley back behind
the dark growl of this old bear den of a bar.

Indizhinikaaz Kwiiwizens,
gaye indizhinikaaz Chi-Ko-ko-koho.
Ni maajaa. Mi-iw. I leave him there.

I am Chi-Ko-ko-koho. I leave him there
under stars of broken glass. I leave him there.

Redemption

After the Great Flood, Nanaboozhoo and four animals floated on a
raft looking for an earth surface on which they could live and walk.
Amik (Beaver), Ojig (Fisher), and Nigiig (Otter) each exhausted their
strengths diving to find where the ground originated, but they were
unable to stay underwater long enough to find the bottom. As they
despaired, the last and smallest animal, Wazhashk (Muskrat) asked to
take a turn. Nanaboozhoo and the other animals told him that is was
hopeless and urged him not to try, but the muskrat insisted on doing
what he could. Because of Wazhashk's courage and sacrifice the earth
was renewed.

Wazhask, the sky watched this.
Mewinzhaa, long before the memory of mortals,
Wazhashk, the sky watched your timid gallant warrior body
>>> deliberate, then plunge
>>>>> with odd grace and dreadful fragility
>>> into translucent black water,
>>> dark mystery unknown and vast as the night sky
and barely (to a single inhalation shared by a weeping four
and a hopeful splash quieter than an oar) break the surface
>>> into concentric expanding disappearing rings as
>>> water circled your departure,
>>> for a moment transparently covering small soles,
>>> tiny seed pearl toes
>>> above that determined small warrior body
>>> that hurtled from sight then
>>> in an instant was pulled into cold dark depths,
>>> seeking the finite in the veins of a waterlocked earth.

Wazhashk, the water covering the earth watched this.
Mewinzhaa, long before the memory of mortals,
Wazhashk, when you were obscured from the sky the water watched
 you
(lost from the sight of the praying four
>>>>> alone on a small raft afloat on vast water)
nearly faint under crushing cold

alone then below the waterline
seeking the finite in the veins of a cumbrous earth
as waterfingers intruded and invaded
all unguarded aspects of your small warrior body
now stiff and graceless
        pulled by will into icy dark depths.

Wazhashk, in that dark mystery
unknown and vast as the night sky
you continued your solitary plunge
        (lost from the sight of all who lived abovewater,
                who considered your size and your courage)
        until in cold and exhaustion your silent voice whispered

        ninzegizi nigiikaj
        nindayekoz niwiinibaa

        I am frightened I am cold
        I am tired I must sleep now

and was heard by the Great Spirit.

Wazhashk, you were heard and were answered

        gawiin ni wi maajaa sin
        gaawin gi ga nogan i sinoon

        have courage, have courage in the darkness
        you are not alone, I am always with you
        have courage, have courage in the darkness

till your spirit roused and spoke

        I hear, I am here, I will try
                through my despair I will

And the Great Spirit watched this and guided you.
Mewinzhaa, long before the memory of mortals
Wazhashk, the Great Spirit guided you, and watched
  your small curled brown fingers
  stretch curving black claws
    to grasp the muddy, rocky breast
    of a waiting Mother Earth.

And today, Wazhashk, hear us breathe,
our inhalations and exhalations a continuing song
of courage sacrifice grace redemption a continuing song
since long before the memory of mortals.
With each telling of the story with each singing of the song
  we once again rise to break the surface and seek
  the finite beyond the grace of this merciful Earth,
  the finite beyond the mercy of this graceful Earth.

Linda LeGarde Grover

The Refugees

To the dirging of "The Way We Were"
sung by some sweet girl nobody knows
six pallbearers
two in sweatshirts with washed-away logos,
three in second-hand dress shirts
one in a borrowed sport coat
carry above a crooked lockstep mince
that flocked vinyl coffin out the side door.
Inside, our beloved mother, grandma and aunt
has left,
has arrived, megis shell on a black string
wound over her hard brown fingers.

Six pallbearers worn as their boot heels
ground to an unassuming humility
by the rounds of looking for work
and sometimes finding it
wear their bodies as a single suit of clothes
fraying fast, and thin at the knees.
Innocents, their faces suncreased by outside labor
and filled, so quickly, by grime and hard living,
spend night after numb night on a stool at Mister Z's
to search then escape what they've found
thinking, maybe after a couple more
I'll ask that blonde or her friend to dance
no, guess I'll just go home, after all.

This is what really happened to the other Indians,
not the New Age beauties you watch on made-for-TV movies,
running in designer loincloths
through a pristine forest full of friendly animals
with an important message from the Chief
and his daughter, the Princess,
the ones who dazzle you today
with their mystical ways

("oh wow you people are just so close to nature,
so spiritual," I've heard you say)
that you can buy at a pow-wow stand
along with some traditional turquoise and silver
jewelry so you can be an Indian, too. You think.

No, we're the other Indians,
the ones who did our time in boarding school,
learned to take a beating,
never quite mastered English
learned the work ethic
and learned what it meant for us,
and chose to survive in spite of it.
Off the reservation, we're refugees,
displaced persons sometimes scorned by our own people.
Our daughters married white men,
learned to take a beating
never quite mastered Anglo housekeeping
lived the work ethic and for them it meant
they would grow old early our *daughters*
beloved and revered the bearers of life
and generations to come how could we protect them,
those slender girls whose bodies tired and whose

blue-eyed children went to public school
and learned to take a beating
or sometimes give one
and never quite mastered schoolwork,
leaving when they turned sixteen,
having learned the work ethic
so they too could live hard
and grow old early.

And today we're at another funeral
and since it's all we could afford
we have to hustle outside The Chapel of the Sunset
once our hour is done. We're grateful, though;
it's warm out today, with room on the sidewalk

Linda LeGarde Grover

for cousins to meet and talk
("haven't seen you since the last funeral")
till the chapel needs the sidewalk back
and we head for Mr. Z's.
The corpse, beloved mother, aunt and grandma
waits, now that she's arrived west,
in the Chapel's garage for a ride to the cemetery
megis shell on a black cord
wound over her hard brown fingers.

Leslie Harper

Region

The day you showed me Isleta pottery
you had to explain to me over
and over
how they burned the design in with horse hair.
I didn't understand
until today when I saw the two
who loved each other under the bridge as secrets.
He was showing her how the rain doesn't fall
like sheets onto our bed,
but in streaks,
which the river quickly erases.
I loved the angles of your body.
I know today you are making a vase of me
only you won't decorate me in circles.
You had this light skin mistaken
for one of the tourist women you sell yourself to.
Now that I am a zagging arrow,
you are afraid my mother's medicine will find its way
out of my spirit
and into your heart's home.
I know
This is how you are
potter.

Leslie Harper

Impasse

You came, a whiteman dressed in thunder
As if I danced for you,

I refused your arrogance.

You spoke of dancing colors
As if you were an honored warrior.

I refused your bragging.

When we buried John in turquoise glory,
You wrapped your arms around me.

I refused to be stifled.

You can't give me boundaries
Like a filmstrip Aborigine.

I refuse you.

Gordon Henry

The Failure of Certain Charms

Dark flows from the memory
of crows, gasping away west
autumn violet at dusk.

Rock loves the Strawberry girl.
I hear his voice when he picks
her up on the two-track behind
the red house, so he knows my
dream of her fragrance
in White Earth wind.

He also knows I carry too
many musical memories
to the gates of the graveyard
under the pines.

This is how it is with me.
I am behind Rock,
a distant flute among gestures
and shadows.

The Strawberry girl loves Rock,
and night spins away
one song, one fragrance
after another.

Gordon Henry

Songs for Sisters
Who Won't Let Go

When Zahquod died
you could not say
Baa maa api

You could not even
raise your eyes to greet
even the most distant
of relatives or the
closest of visitors.

You left silence between
yourself and the Northern Oriole
singing over sections
of orange on the rail
beneath the thermometer
face.

You turned instead
from memory to memory
to find memory always
behind or awaiting another
present of some sensual
association like a luminous
guide hollowing a place
for us out of this good
earth.

Outside White Earth

Vision and breath
travel away in
the smell of rain.
Next to a pickup
an old man stands
sleeping drunk,
hand on zipper.
    Leave him.
There is the liquor store.
Jukebox shadows of music
coming back around again
and again.
Torrents of faces
and women
shapes of smoke
opening mouths opening
restroom doors almost
as frequently.

At the touch of a hand
leaving, rain fills
your ears from the
roof, crumbling you
awake. You
stand,
    hand on zipper,
face against a phone
number
on the paint
of a peeling wall.

Gordon Henry

How Soon

The story goes from in a rainfall
to sister walking a field in autumn.
And when she arrives
winter has come, so the old man
rises from his chair, picks up
matches, pipe and tools, and
walks out to begin again.

The sculptures grow by the day,
birds in ice, recognizable
eagles, a bear that began
as a man in a moment of dance.
He does this in ice, all
winter carving at dawn,
carving at dusk.

And sister after walking a field
browned autumn arrives, watches
from the east window, waits,
goes out to him in spring,
taps him on the shoulder,
and points to the pools
of water he's standing over.

Remembering Shadow:
the art of not crying

Comedic voices
like moonlight
better than bar
signs.

The clown pose
leaves once you
succumb to the
medication.

So your woman's
a Mormon Angel
who gave you a
boy called shadow.

Gaygoo maw wee kay
gay goo mish shee shay

Remember the passing
train a twisting doppler
crescendo lip sync
sermon of some latter
day saint speak.

Remember the early white moon
as we sang

gaygoo naw waw paw mee ko wah
bee nee shay

from the thirsty dance
cycle and watched
shadows go
into the ground.

Gordon Henry

Dodem Dream Song

Old Man
I will guide your silver canoe
to the center of the water
where the Loon Father carries
children on his back.

If I am quiet
I will arrive as a call
from another shore
to draw close enough
to see the fantastic eyes
seeing me drifting
alone.

Al Hunter

Prayer Bowl

When the moon is turned upwards like a bowl waiting to be filled
We must fill it. We must fill it by honouring the spirits of creation
With songs of our joy and thanks, with foods created from our own hands,
Water for the thirsty, prayers for the people, prayers for spirits,
Prayers for the Creator, prayers for ourselves, and the sacred instruments
That join us to the glory of this world, that join us to the glory of this world
And the world beyond our sleep.

Al Hunter

In Neah Bay
for Spirit Horse

1.
To say that there are words to describe the feelings of the ocean would
be to
lie. To
use a language that would describe one ounce of ocean wave would be
to
speak the
tongue yet to be spoken. There are no words.

horses in my heart.
horses in my heart.

2.
From the farthest northwest corner of this island,
of this continent, the blue sea—
emerald tides and waves of jade,
touching and caressing ancient faces of the land.
I dream of you. I think of you. I remember you.

Poem for Patrick Eller

A tattered chapbook with a wolf and three moons—
"the sky full of miracles and everyone is sleeping . . ."

One of the three moons, the largest one, encircles the image
of a bird in flight. The wolf stares off as the second moon
touches his right ear.

The other moon rests over his back, suspended, in the night sky.

Are you the flying bird inside the blue ring of the shining moon?
Are you one of these moons? Which moon are you?
The voice whispering into the ear of the wolf?
The waiting moon above the forest?

Al Hunter

Jailer

This cage of flesh
and bone
needs cleaning.
The shadow of the jailer
looms behind me.

Another One of Those Skeletons in the Closet

Reaching out with hands of bone,
bleached bare and barren of skin,
reaching out, only scratching the surface,
pointing bony fingers to an empty chest,
motioning thirstily to parched, exposed remains,
for a thirst that can never be quenched,
for an empty cage,
for which no escape could ever sate,
for which no escape could ever sate,
for which no escape could ever sate.

Blue Horses

My lover gave me a turquoise-blue horse.
I held her in my outstretched arms and I wept.
For so long I have waited for you, I whispered.
For so long I have dreamed of you, I confided.
For so long I have sung without you, I chanted.
For so long I have prayed without you, I murmured.
For so long I have walked without you,
I breathed.

Leanne Flett Kruger

Brother Wolf
(visit to the zoo)

paws pacing
endless fenceline
in a four by six cell
barren eyes
spirit lost
        . . . are you still there?

breathing, panting
placid, flaccid,
pale grey tongue
hangs from mouth
rotting teeth
no longer tear
living flesh
feeding life into you

meals served, not hunted
spoiled meat, stagnant water
you will die here
pacing worn paws
is waste

do you hope?
do you still dream?
to return to your birthplace
        your migratory roots
        your ancestral grounds
        to hunt
        to be free

. . . I pray you still hope
and somehow it may offer your spirit
some ease

Leanne Flett Kruger

like my own people
my poor Brother
I cry for you
your absent howl
echoes your genocide

in empty territories
claimed Terra Nulluis*
by greedy men
who created the
desecration
of wolves

Note: Terra Nullius in this poem is pertaining to the residence of Wolves rather than people.

Terra Nullius, a land that is empty of people.
*This is the legal concept used by Europeans when they first arrived in North America. They wanted to justify their claim to all the land, pretending that no one else had been here first.
—From "People of Terra Nullius" by Boyce Richardson

Sweat

clean out the lodge
smell of boughs
rocks on the fire
going inside
back into the womb
of mother earth

cold ground on my naked feet and knees
as i gently feel my way
around the circle

the darkness of the womb
the blackness of the lodge
breathing deep
thick moist air

sounds of sizzle and spit
as medicine water hits
hot stones

the dense dark mist
sweat dripping down
my face

clear my mind
as breathing relaxes
prayers from within
find their way
to my voice
in song
in word
in moans

songs fill me
songs from my elders
as drum rhythms beat in my head

Leanne Flett Kruger

the drumbeat in my spirit
the heartbeat in the womb
shed my skin
and bones
nourish my spirit
with prayers
as the ancestors cradle me
and sing to me
back in the womb
of mother earth

Jamison Mahto

The Blue Apache

We used to have a lot of fun;
a twelve pack of Budweiser,
pack of Camel straights,
and a drum;
singing those high and lovely songs
on the top of Black Bear Butte;
we danced smilin' around a fire
and wished this night would last forever.

You could share the blanket
with the raven haired Choctaw woman
in the jingle dress,
and sleep the sleep when you dream your power,
and you could dream those dreams that keep all men young.

I was young and tight
and I feared nothing;
I understood freedom and dignity and honor.

The bunch of us would sweat and pray together;
we would hunt and fish;
everyone would feast
and the elders ate first.

Sometimes we would hotwire a Camaro;
drive it until it wouldn't go any farther.

Sometimes we would raid the ranches
at the edge of the reservation ghetto
and butcher the beef behind Anna Mae's barn.

Jamison Mahto

Wovoka and a sixteen-year-old ghost dancer;
buckskin strength and 60 million buffalo memories
celebrate an ancient echo
amid the architecture of desperation;
set loose in the urban reservation
down the path of righteous profanity and glorious suicide.

I was so young;
the damage was done
for a few moments
of intricate chance
with a tube of glue,
a jug of whiskey,
pills in a jar,
junk in a rig,
the angry needle in your veins,
your spiritual radar rendered useless;
wino park your camp on the avenue;
felt hats and feathers
in a funky rock-n-roll jungle;
the world unbalanced
and the past my narcotic;
my identity a main nerve explosion of delight;
an evangelical fanaticism
of beadwork and jewelry and lost languages.

The dude had a gun,
he was crazy out of it;
I did the only thing I could;
I hit 'im across the back of the head
with the war club chair;
how was I to know that he was gonna hemorrhage
lying there on the floor at my feet;
lying there on that barroom floor;
he had a gun;
and it was pointed at my best friend.

Jamison Mahto

I was young and bad
and jail was my teacher

I exchanged my cell
for lyin' face down in a rice paddy;
hot lead whistlin' overhead;
smellin' death mud and napalm.
It was an easy choice.

I came home to Alcatraz and Wounded Knee;
they circled the church with APC's;
helicopters, night fighting technology,
Hotchkiss guns on the hill,
against one AK-47, our .22's, hunting rifles,
shotguns, bows and arrows.

Crawling on our bellies;
warriors on the rise;
I know how to spell victory;
you'll have to cut my legs off at the joint
to get me to kneel!

Grandfathers and fathers and sons
praying for the spirits of the ancestors
and the survival of the living.

Grandmothers and mothers and daughters
singing for the unborn;
wailing, lonely and sad;
could'ja dig the history of it!

Jamison Mahto

I am the people.
I am the historical schizophrenia.
I am the four directions. I am Opechancanough
leading a rebellion, almost a hundred years old,
almost blind, almost kicked some English butt
back into the ocean.
we wouldn't have had to bother,
if we hadn't fed them,
if we hadn't helped them survive
through the hard years, those first cold hard years.

I am the truth;
Sand Creek, Washita,
Black Elk,
Rolling Thunder, Sitting Bull, Crazy Horse,
Laramie Treaty, Treaty Of Medicine Lodge.

I am Joe Boneclub;
pissed his pants
standin' at the street corner bus stop,
diggin' round for spare change
and cigarette butts.

we are the landlords
and the rent is way past due . . .

I am the center of the universe;
call me the Blue Apache.

Litany II

—from deep in the valley of the
shadow of death—

this morning
new york
in loss of innocence
was given voice,
the screaming jerky crack babies of Harlem,
the bag lady from Brooklyn,
the junkie in the doorway,
the alley,
the boarded up tenement temple
where sacraments are shared,
our dancing hearts
are exhausted, yet,
all our tired souls
can sing,
just sing,
thanks . . .

thanks, man,
for this tobacco,
rolling papers,
cuppa coffee,
and the strength
to keep putting one foot
in front of another . . .

thanks for this morning,
exact and perfect,
in its violence and destruction,
in its beauty and courage,
in its lust and greed,
in its lies and scams and two-bit video schemes,
in its birth and promise and dreams,
ahhhhh, yes,
the dawn . . .

thanks are given
to tunkasila
for rain
or tears
or a day
at the beach,
for cleansing sweat and the pain of breath,
thanks for reggae,
country,
and jazz.
thanks for rock-n-roll
for without it,
I would surely be dead
yet, I am here,
yes, hoka hey, yes.
thanks to this dawn,
this foggy gray morning,
thanks, great mystery
for music and my Sony walkman.

tunkasila,
bless the mad gunman,
celebrate the deaths and screams
in New Orleans
as the fires
of summer
burn wildly
out of control;
thanks, god,
for drive-by shootings,
bless the innocent bystander
whose number was up!

thanks for
blood and semen,
fluids and pheromones,
sweat drenched bed sheets
and lips swept away in passionate kissing.
there could never be

tenderness,
kindness,
or understanding
without b.b. king and Lucille,
and I would be truly lost in this jungle
without the passion of Carlos Santana
becoming one with an electric guitar.

thanks, tunkasila,
for these perfect hands and feet,
for my perfect mind,
my spare tire,
my gray hair,
a good bowel movement
and the blues.

thanks, baby,
for l.a.,
Hollywood and sunset;
dig it, man,
the dark evil death
lurking behind the tv set.
we give thanks for
brando,
James dean,
and Marilyn;
thank you for
trust,
hello,
and yes.
tunkasila, we give thanks
for mahto,
victory at little big horn,
women and children
and horses
where sat these great warriors,
thanks for this holy night
electric and alive with neon.

we give thanks for Minneapolis avenues
late at night,
shelters for the homeless
and branch 1.

I have heard the voice of the prophet
Joe paper,
"15-2, 15-4, 15-6,
and a pair for 8"!
yeah, man,
we give thanks for the cribbage board and cards,
and games that kept me sane
through 58 days on the county side
in the old Hennepin courthouse jail.
oh, painful, lustful soul
thou hast cried such tears
was made joyful
with the birth of a daughter;
we give thanks for
library cards,
cable access,
all night radio dj's
and smokin' some thundershit
on the lightning lit back porch
quietly with friends,
pulling me back
from the edge
of madness
with firm caring grace.

tunkasila, hear me!
smaller than a neutrino,
let my voice fill your universe
with singing,
with singing I am filled
and overflowing
with the Mississippi,
this moon,

with this alleluia,
with this whispering alleluia.
every step I take
is the right path
because I am here
now!

holy is this moment
this moment, this moment.
holy is this rain,
holier than the holiest of holies
like holy Paha Sapa on a futon in the autumn.
holy is this perfect moment,
this sublime and beautiful madness
has got me by the throat
and just won't let go.

Joyce carlEtta Mandrake

Rest Home

Rest home for the aged.
No rest, from the moaning, swearing in the hall,
Damn it, Damn it.

Damn it, a life that winds down like this.
A friend's legs are broken
Torn by a steel monster
She is banished to this place

Today, her roommate cried,
placed back in her bed, I wept inside.
Longed to hold her, to rock her, to coo,
"You can not be forgotten."

There is a child here
sitting in a wheelchair.
His joy is in the morning;
he goes to school.
Returning in the afternoon to the moaning, swearing in the hall,
Damn it, Damn it.

My mother died there
twenty-four years ago.
My tears are still here, hiding in my throat,
in another rest home for the aged.
Damn it, Damn it . . .

Values

I feel like I was cheated
Because I wasn't born an Indian,
An old white woman says to me.

Cheated out of what?

Your tribal lands,
Sacred ceremonies,
Language?

Yes, you were cheated
I say nothing.

Joyce carlEtta Mandrake

Dream Sequence

Hunting with cougar
On the mountainside
In my four-footed coat
Humanity hidden.

Black bear chasing me
Through a many-leveled lodge
He chases me, shouting,
"Now is the time to learn."

In dream I am eagle and soar
Wind rushing through wings
As I fly higher and higher
Up into my father sky.

Walking with Buffalo Woman,
Wrapped in her white robes.
The circle of life is our vision,
Elders in death, rising again in life.

In dreams, I have danced
With vision teachings, spirits calling;
Helping me in my life.

Rasunah Marsden

Dancing the Rounds

this page & I dance by lamplight in nights
before modern conveniences
I join hands with the ancestors
who jigged & drank
thru log cabin living rooms
in the rugged bays of lakesides
whose tree-scraped skies
were cluttered with the spirits of World Wars
& I join hands with all the brown-eyed children lost
or abused and the families whose spirits
are still being broken by anger & greed

by the shadowy flicker of lamplight
I step gingerly over borders centuries old
& watch the repetitive fall of kingdoms
& the lives of princes and saints unfold;
in fields of revelation unceasing
exquisite orchids grow

as I drive to this valley
ringed with the history of desert survival
loved ones past and present recede,
recede into landscape,
are submerged in memory—
so many leaves under snow,

the wake of creation,
is littered with the detritus
of what we are: as under a lens,
still transparencies,
(or only so many hurled stars);
are traced onto the page, fleetingly
until it is folded & yellowed

Rasunah Marsden

in the dance of worlds
the pulse of her blood thru our hearts
enlivens the play of words

in time which sanctifies or existence which typifies
the natural illumination of all things, between particles
of dust which permeate the air we breathe,
between shadows irradiated by lamplight on the screen,
dust, leaves, stars scatter, are folded away

Tossing Around

that orchid's other-worldly
grows fastened onto a certain tree,
blooms only on special nights,
you need to watch for it or you'll miss it
& the other way that orchid weaves its spell
is to inseminate all within reach
with its exotic odor, so drop everything
you're doing, that orchid's there
to be admired, incandescently glowing
near the goldfish pond,
just YOU don't forget what it takes
to care for that orchid
or you'll writhe in pain
with what it is capable of suffering
something about that orchid
I'm still tossing around

that crow he's a black fool
hanging around, making lots of noise
pushing his crowbeak between your fingers feeding,
but you can bet he'll be first
to graze on your innards
should you decline in strength, that crow
knows exactly what he's up to
just YOU don't forget what he wants
or he'll be gone
something about that crow
I'm still tossing around

Rasunah Marsden

The Best Medicine

when dona bellisimo's genuine masterpiece
went tick tock & she woke up
between the lines, the world went running
to her door. She wakes up to heart
beats
& every other thing you can see
below the balconies miraculously
leaves you unscathed: thieves shatter
a window and bleed when they yank out
a stereo; or just as equivocally distressed
some other crowd disperses madly
when gunshots fly overhead just as amazingly
& you are unimpressed

this could be anywhere, but it's not
so let us have this conversation
in a burning world about days
when people cared about the bodies
they left behind & creators knew
to avoid what was mundane
like the plague. dona bellisimo
wakes up to heart
beats
& you don't know what world
is flying by anymore between the scalpel's
edge & the bodies of prophets
whose wounds from stem to stern
were closed in the longest, bloodiest
agonies in the memories of mankind.
shaking her hair she still hears the wind
whistling thru their rattling teeth
in the hollows of her throat each night

this madness which afflicts, this touch
of brilliance which sparks the mind
& hurls your body thru a door,
has sent dona bellisimo's genuine masterpiece
into the ecstasies of oblivion. I can prove it
to you. Last seen she hung out back
of a gypsy caravan selling a foul smelling
tonic for unmanageable women
which caused a conflagration
which spread over the world. no one
dared to think what they had drunk
nor asked, but like dona bellisimo read
between the lines

of the arrest of a woman
in long black tresses
whose hysterical laughter
caused a public menace
which could be heard in every marketplace
in the world. her only defense,
it was rumored, was this:
"a child who runs thru a field
does not ask why the crickets
who live there sing. She runs,
they sing, the sun's rays uplift us
& I feel no separation
from any heart
beat."

Rene Meshake

The Grand Entry

The Spirits asked, "Who are you?"
I replied
"I'm an Aboriginal."

They said, "Who?"
I answered again,
"I'm a First Nation."

They said, "Who?"
I retorted,
"I'm a Native Canadian."

They said, "Who?"
Finally, it dawned on me
and I proclaimed, "I'm Anishinabe,
Mz aye, indoodem
Dyoosh indanishinabe-bimaadiz."

One of the Spirits acknowledged,
"Biindigen, gichi Anishinabe.
Truly, any Anishinabe who still speaks the language
makes a grand entry in the prayer world."

The Race to the Wiigiwaam

I clutched a birchbasket in one hand,
and a gourd in the other.
I couldn't move.
The wiigiwaam faced me only a few feet away.

With the sunset on my back,
I watched as the shadows grew longer.

The shadow of the birch basket
reached the doorway of the wiigiwaam,
and entered.
But the shadow of the gourd
went past the birchbark-enshrouded lodge
and joined the darkening forest.

Outside the lodge,
I cowered in the dark,
my knuckles turned numb
and the cold buffeted my whole body.

When I looked up,
the Big Dipper sparkled. But I soon discovered that
the stars in the sky were holes
through the roof of the wiigiwaam.

Rene Meshake

Oodena: The Heartbeat of the Anishinabeg

Our pulses raced at the sight of a blond Autumn mosquito;
now only the red leaves will plummet on us.
Our cold fingers grew hot as we paddled along.
I thought only of the hunt ahead.

Jingle Dancer

If you're too exquisite,
I won't disrupt your plans.

If you're too plain,
I won't trouble your heart.

Let's pray that the sound of your jingles
will soon drown out my misgivings,
so that I can fall in step with you.

Rene Meshake

Two Buttons

In my bawaajige dream,
my friends sent me to see a tyrant.
There were two buttons like Siamese twins
inside his windowless heart.
I severed one button
and donated one of mine.

I awoke to see,
in many days, the first sunshine.

Cheryl K. Minnema

Bottled Rage

Wrestled steps stagger with the tall
weeds beside our house.
Another swig of vodka bleeds words
about his girlfriend a half mile down the road,
her bruised cheek pressed against their three children.
Worn tennis shoes rattle the front door.
In the closet, my lip aches between my teeth.
He kicks harder, "Ma let me in."
She is afraid to move.
Bangs harder on the window, I cover my ears.
Alcohol gushes from his stomach.
It's our fault, it's always our fault.
Glass shatters.
Mom is torn from bed.
She fumbles by the phone too late.
Coffee table flips to its back,
chairs crumble from the wall,
counter knickknacks fly,
buried pain spills to the floor.
An officer extends his hand,
he takes it only to ask for another dollar.
Just one, that's all I need.
Thirty years,
one dollar at a time.

Cheryl K. Minnema

Ask Me Who I Am

I will tell you.
Dull aches in your heavy chest.
Cold tears in your swollen eyes.
Lingering voices in your lost mind.
Ask me who I am.
I will tell you.
Cracking of ice beneath you.
Breaking of a limb above you.
Scraping of a fall beside you.
Ask me who I am.
I will tell you.
The rattle of your broken window.
The clink of your rusted chime.
The sway of your empty swing.
Ask me who I am.
I will tell you.
The deepness of that lake.
The current of that river.
The rage of that rapid.
Come closer.
I will show you
who I am.

Paulette Molin

Froggy Pond Memories

for Rena, through thick and thin

The men's skates we found in the guildhall rummage
were way too big for our little girls' feet,
but we put on socks and more socks
in any color or size to try to make them fit.

We envisioned twirling, gliding, and figure-eighting
on the river to Froggy Pond,
but had to struggle to keep our giant skates upright
as we lurched along the slippery path from home.

We slid down bumpy snowbanks at the river,
mostly on our backsides,
pulling each other up when we hit the ice,
only to fall down again and again.

We sometimes chanced into misery at Froggy,
teased by a mean boy,
whose meaner dog once bit you,
making us ever-vigilant to their whereabouts.

Remember, too, the fall through ice-cracking waters,
long coat, big skates, and all.
A miserable human icicle and her sister,
trudging home, full of tearful humiliation.

Reaching the house,
we probed at the frozen, frayed shoelaces
on our rummage skates,
finally unpeeling layer after layer of soggy socks
by the woodburning warmth of the barrel stove.

Paulette Molin

Gull Lake

Before White Earth, there was Gull Lake,
still the sheltering place for graves
our Anishinaabe ancestors wept to leave
on treaty-driven removals
to negotiated promised lands.

Paulette Molin

Riding on Rims

Don't let that noise scare you.
It's just someone riding on rims
on the highway of life.

Paulette Molin

For the Passengers on the Indian Bus

We sat together in the back rows
of your bordertown classrooms,
silent and uncomfortable,
until alphabetical chance scattered us
among boys and girls possessing
white skin privilege and numerical advantage.

Our separateness stood out,
not only in our physical selves,
clothed in garments too big, too small, or too wrong,
but in our woodsmoked presence
and reservation ways.
Native weeds in immigrant fields.

Spilling from the "Indian bus,"
actually golden as any,
on rides to and from school,
we withdrew into turtle-tough shells,
exploded into swearing, bloody fistfights,
or skipped right into reform school.

In whatever seat or row we occupied,
we learned to see ourselves through your eyes,
unwanted and inferior, damaged goods.
We minded this daily lesson,
as we dropped out of your school in droves.

Jim Northrup

Shrinking Away

Survived the war but was having
trouble surviving the peace,
couldn't sleep more than two hours
was scared to be without a gun
nightmares, daymares, guilt and remorse
wanted to stay drunk all the time
1966 and the V.A. said
Vietnam wasn't a war
they couldn't help but did
give me a copy of the Yellow Pages
picked a shrink off the list
50 bucks an hour
I was making 125 a week
Spent six sessions establishing rapport
heard about his military life
his homosexuality, his fights with his mother
and anything else he wanted to talk about
At this rate, we would have got to me in 1999
Gave up on that shrink, couldn't afford him
and he wasn't doing me any good.
Six weeks later my shrink killed
himself—Great
Not only guilt about the war but
new guilt about my dead shrink
If only I had a better job
I could have kept on seeing him
I thought we were making real progress
Maybe in another six sessions I could
have helped him.
I realized then that
surviving the peace was up to me.

Jim Northrup

Manoomin

Tobacco swirled in the lake
as we offered our thanks
The calm water welcomed us
rice heads nodded in agreement
Ricing again, mii gwech Manido
Cedar caressed the heads
ripe rice came along to join us
in many meals this winter
The rice bearded up
We saw the wind move across the lake
an eagle, a couple of coots
the sun smiled everywhere
Relatives came together
talk of other lakes, other seasons
fingers stripping rice while
laughing, gossiping, remembering
Its easy to feel a part of
the generations that have
riced here before
It felt good to get on the lake
It felt better getting off
carrying a canoe load of food
and centuries of memories

Lifetime of Sad

She's 50, alone and drunk
She has pride in her language
but no one to talk to
Some don't understand
Some can't, some won't
She's buried two husbands
warriors in the white man's war
Her children are raised and gone
a five year battle with cancer
a longer battle with the bottle
She's broke and 50 miles from her empty bed
alcohol failed her, she's too drunk
to talk, but not drunk enough to pass out
Her eyes show a lifetime of sad
She cried out for beer, smokes,
attention or affection
She only got the attention
when she was caught stealing food
from the house she was visiting
She was asked to leave
She left, 50, alone, and drunk

Jim Northrup

Wiigwaas

Time to gather bark
another gift from the Creator
Just doing what grampa did
like his grampa before him
went with a cousin I've known
since we ate oatmeal from the same bowl
mosquitoes and deer flies welcomed
us to their feast
A sparrow hawk flew by
supper in his feet
Watched a deer feeding
in the lake shallows
Each tree leads to others
farther from the road
Found one that's been waiting
sixty years to become a basket
A cut allows the bark to
crack, crack open
Hands slipped inside
feel the smooth wet
the bark jumps from the tree
eager to help us
make a basket or two
Finally we have enough bark
it was time to go home
we were getting hungry

Ogichidaa

I was born in war, WW Two
Listened as the old men told stories
of getting gassed in the trenches, WW One
Saw my uncles come back from
Guadalcanal, North Africa and
the Battle Of The Bulge
Memorized the war stories
my cousins told of Korea
felt the fear in their voices
finally it was my turn
my brothers too
Joined the Marines in time
for the Cuban Missile Crisis
Heard the crack of rifles in
the rice paddies south of Da Nang
Saw my friends die there
then tasted the bitterness of
the only war America ever lost
My son is now a warrior
Will I listen to his stories
Or cry into his open grave?

Jim Northrup

Wahbegan

Didja ever hear a sound
smell something
taste something
that brought you back to
Vietnam, instantly?
Didja ever wonder
when it would end?
It ended for my brother
he died in the war
but didn't fall down
for fifteen tortured years
his flashbacks are over
another casualty whose name
will never be on the Wall
some can only find peace in death
The sound of his family crying hurt
The smell of the flowers
didn't comfort us
The taste in my mouth
still sours me
How about a memorial
for those who made it
through the war
but still died
before their time

Lisa Poupart

Clorox Treatment

Standing above my father
three and a half feet tall

carried home from a bar floor
after playing softball

immobile in bed
face bruised and purple
Alcohol seeps from his pores

A crazy glued virgin mary statue
on the night stand
next to his head
her back turned away

Drunk and incoherent
Begs my mother for forgiveness
Swollen lips
Slurred speech
weeping
weeping
"Rosie, honey
we had to fight those white guys
said things about Indians"

Eyes
rolling back
into his head

Standing above my father
three and a half feet tall

She
reminds me in shame and disgust
"This is what it means to be an Indian—
Drunk. And baby, you're an Indian"

Lisa Poupart

While
all she can think is
"I'm the one who has to clean his
goddamned ball uniform"

Bleach out
     the red blood
         brown dirt
             invisible tears

Like she wished she could
bleach out
his dark skin
as white as her own

Inheritance

When he was a small boy he tried
to summon the spirits with a flute
that his father threw out the window
while promptly beating his face in

On the bus to the big school
the white kids called him
timber nigger
he learned the only good indian is a dead one
unless he plays ball

So he learned to run and tackle
to cheer the onlookers
till his father stabbed a hole in the pigskin
while promptly breaking the foot that he kicked with

Then he started to drink blue ribbon
smashed his head through windshields
numbing the pain of an existence
too aching to bear

And
somewhere between two and nineteen
he turned hollow and dried up
his spirit flew off to the west

His body now a shell left behind him
to carry out revenge
for five hundred years of genocide
eaten out of an empty government hand-out can

When he put the rifle to his wife's head
and raped his two babies
he never even felt it
because he was already dead

Marcie Rendon

native love

somethin' about dark skin
brown eyes that shift to black during lovemaking or a fight
braids tangled, his and yours
afterwards
tracing the denim-blue eagle tattooed on his left arm
"where'd you get this?"
"stillwater."
or marion or sandstone
the quick and easy grin that lets you know that the world's all right
right now
"how's the curves girl?"
no insult intended
you always know that your place is the place
chances are he doesn't have his own
no game playing decisions to make at last call, last song,
last inter-tribal
your place, always your place
when they say they want to take you home
you know where they're coming from
they always want to know if you're married
not cause they care about takin another man's wife
most likely they just want to avoid the fight
or have a really good one
indian men
they know how to make love quiet
no need to explain to them about not wakin up the kids
they know
mis-matched sheets and star-quilts
maybe in the winter the orange-red pendleton
they let you smoke after sex
drink cold coffee sittin on the edge of the bed
bare feet danglin to the floor
they listen to your dreams in the morning
tell you what their grandma told them 'bout what dreaming 'bout
  tornados means

indian men
short, tall, prison hard, or fry-bread soft
they don't talk much
but it is true, they are good with their hands.
i've fallen in love with a man's hips leaning into the bar railing
another's hands carving pipestone into prayer
one man's bank of the eight ball into the last pocket
one christmas i watched a man grass dance at a sobriety pow-wow
when my girlfriend asked, "what do you want for christmas?"
i pointed with my lips
she laughed
he's been gone for years
but his daughter hip-hops in my living room
her easy grin and smooth moves a lasting memory
of a christmas gift i asked for and got
i don't think i've ever fallen out of love
they move on or i need space
but i can't help falling in love
someone's grin, another's eyes
the way one holds a rifle in the woods
or poles rice in the fall
and a good laugh
or a flirting 49 will get me every time.

Marcie Rendon

solitary silence

in solitary silence
   i heard rain sigh and
the autumn moon rise
      singing love songs through fields of golden wheat
in solitary silence
i heard the satin glide of fog across a morning lake
   and dew giggle as it's tickled by the sun
in solitary silence
   i heard my baby's first breath
     corn grow
       and flowers burst
alone
i watched the grand canyon eat the sun
the smokies swallow dusk
    and a pebbled stream give birth to a mighty river
      her final scream was muted in a louisiana bayou
alone
the atlantic begged me to join him
     lapping up my legs to my thighs
  jealous
the pacific roared
threatened me with harm if i didn't do her bidding
in solitary silence
     the creator rocked me in the arms of a cottonwood
    while maple trees murmured and jackpines snored
      their rumbling/grumbling keeping nightmares at bay
in solitary silence
   i have waited to hear
    dawn break
     quasars pulse
in solitary silence
   i waited
until
   the crow said all is well
   and the nighthawk walked me gently home

my child's hunger

my child's hunger keeps me company
working all night
fingers turned raw from spools of thread wound too tight
trying to gain an extra yard
from a spool not meant to stretch that far
my child's future stitched into high-fashioned seams
working all night
an extra dollar made

my child's hunger keeps me company
working all night
in an outfit made from spools of thread wound too tight
a soul's not meant to stretch this far
in too-tight, too-high, high-heeled shoes
slipping off the edge of the world
is what i do best
　　working all night
　　an extra dollar made

aching bodies
sell dreams
exchanging expendable commodities
for an extra dollar made

working evening shifts
graveyard time/midnight dust
holds dreams alive

Marcie Rendon

grandmother walks.....

grandmother walks moonlit trails
sucking maple syrup cubes
birchbark wraps itself around her
while black bear guards her path

at the water's edge,
in a rock upon the path,
flickering in an evening flame
i see her face

flying into denver

flying into denver
i dreamt of you
it was a dream that stretched across the straight-line horizon
two hours and thirty minutes long

at the airport
i rushed outside to touch the first snowflake of the year
   it melted on my cheek
     reminiscent of a kiss placed there by you

flying west
   i saw your face in a mountain canyon
     Plexiglas and thirty-thousand feet of airspace
     prevented me from reaching you

in seattle
  —displaced—
i stood alone on a concrete corner
   cold air wrapped around me

a bronzed and chiseled man approached
   "sister can you spare some change?"
       i imagine tlinglet whaling boats and raven totem
poles as his rolling walk, dollar bill in fisted hand,
      takes him to the corner liquor store
across the street
   a weathered vendor sells me a single red flower with a hundred
     loves me/loves-me-not/loves me/loves-me-not petals

in a Starbucks coffee cup vase
i pretend it's you
sitting on a chair by this king-size bed
taking the edge
off this lonely chill

Armand Garnet Ruffo

Rockin' Chair Lady
(for Alice)

Today's the day I wake up knowing I'm going to commit myself
to the memory of Mildred Bailey. To my young mother
spinning her unfashionable and unpardonable jazzy 78's
(in the land of Country & Western)
on her rigged-up gramophone. Music
I couldn't appreciate, let alone understand.

These days an old woman I met out west years ago
sends me tapes from her collection
spanning seventy years. The last one of Bix Beiderbecke,
the white cornet player from the 1920s
(they say he sounded like a girl saying yes)
who played black and died at twenty-eight. Bootlegged
booze and passion will do that.

As for Mildred, the encyclopedia says
she was "The first white singer to absorb
and master the jazz-flavored phrasing, enunciation,
embellishments, improvisatory fervor,
and swinging rhythm of her black contemporaries."
To put it plainly, "the first non-black woman
to sing jazz convincingly."

What they don't say is that she was Indian,
Coeur d'Alene to be exact,
and could party with the best of them.
In jazz things are either black or white.
Red doesn't count. Unless your name is
Red Norvo, the musician Mildred lived with
for twelve years, before she got too fat and too sick.
Diabetes (the Indian disease) and heart trouble,
or trouble of the heart, claimed her in '51,
before I was even born.

But back to Mildred's young life. Bound for the city,
she got a job with the Paul Whiteman Orchestra
(talk about ironic) and hit the jazz scene
big time, in a world of big band swing.
They called her the Rockin' Chair Lady
because she was one great swinger
who sang with the greats, Goodman,

               Dorsey,

               Hodges,

               Hawkins, to name a few,
and took over the airwaves on her own national show.

Imagine tuning into her voice
on your Motorola. Hot stuff in 1933.
Imagine being labeled Indian back then
and not wanting to be, because red is out,
it doesn't count,
and hearing Mildred
coming in strong, knowing she's in
all the way to the top.

Armand Garnet Ruffo

At Geronimo's Grave

Fierce, tenacious, master of guerilla warfare.

It's what the history books say. Though
at his grave, out of an unyielding sun,
and into a sanctuary of leafy shade, I move
through all that is said, and not said,
and touch the flowers left for him,
which make me wonder if it is possible for anyone
to have the last word. And I am reminded
that it took five thousand troops to track down
what was left of his Apache, thirty-five
men, women and children. Caught.
They say herded from New Mexico to Florida to Alabama
and finally all the way here to Oklahoma, to so-called
Indian territory (as if the rest of the country wasn't).

They say more.

That by the time he died at eighty he had embraced Christianity
and even taken part in a Presidential inauguration.
Part of the parade I suspect, the evidence committed
to memory: last year in England, at the Brighton Museum
(of all places), I bought a postcard of him lost
behind the wheel of a Model T Ford,
looking like he had just fallen out of the sky and
onto the driver's seat. Portrait of an old Chief in a top hat.
(It was my only purchase.) From there to here in one fatal swoop
as though giant talons have dropped me unexpectedly
onto this site. If I could I would ask him
if he too got plucked up by something larger than himself.

Last of the hold-outs, they call him.

This morning at Fort Sill I saw the windowless cellar
they held him in (not open to the public)
and the other building they transferred him to,
the one turned into a museum and whitewashed.
A notice said he really spent little time in his cell
since he had the run of the place,
like a bed and breakfast, I am led to believe.
Yet, with wilted petals between my fingers soft as grace,
soft as old sorrow, and an even older sun overhead
guiding me beyond this arbor and back onto the highway,
I am left wondering about who he really was.
Oilfields and prairie flowers, barbed wire and distant mesas
red as a people locked behind aging vision
telling me it is the land that will have the last word.

For him whom they also call Prisoner of War.

Armand Garnet Ruffo

Bear

A young woman crawls into his bed
warms it golden in the late afternoon.
He returns after a day's outing,
stealing honey, munching ants,
causing general ruckus.

Then, again, perhaps he's home from school.

He opens the door only to find her
scattered clothes
which he trails to her body.
She has come to be devoured.
Every morsel.

So he begins with toes, feet, moves to leg
up inside of thigh.
When he gets to the tenderest part,
she whimpers for him
to stop.

She is losing herself to his bare kiss.

But the moment he does, she whispers,
to go on. And he does,
as though together
they were retelling
an old-time story.

Blueberries

The end of summer
and we pick blue
berries, pluck them
with delicate precision,
        open ourselves to the goodness
        of the world
        that is theirs
drop the offering
onto our ready tongues
and drift into heavy clouds
bringing us to remember

friends who move
marry
make pies and jam
they ate as children for their own children,
holding to the sweetness
they once loved.

and divorced
that's them too
when fingers cramp, stop,
mouths close in denial,
and the heart's want
is replaced by the sickly feeling
of having too much
too little.

Armand Garnet Ruffo

But here kneeling in the ruins
of stumps as far as the eye can see,
we take these berries,
blue as the new life they are,
      in gratitude
      humility,
      yet lustful for the taking.
The dusty logging road at our backs
we stand, stretch to leave
at day's end
and laugh in our full desire
all the way home.

Drum Song

I write words like justice, obligation,
responsibility, treaty, suicide.
And shout them from the rooftop.
My neighbours who are in their garden,
look up and conveniently ignore me.
They think I'm drunk,
but I haven't touched a drop.
The bottle I'm holding
is actually a homemade bomb,
a poetry bomb,
that will soon shower
the sky with words
they can no longer ignore.

In the archives, another photograph of a treaty expedition, more white collars and Union Jacks. Even on this spring day, the old air of officialdom pervades, dry as August's dead heat. The commissioners dominate the page (their faith and loyalty to king and country holding them steadfast) flanked by military men, equally stiff and formal, as though on guard. For what? For whom? For you grandfather? In case you caught on to what was actually going on, what they were actually up to and tried to stop them, did something foolish—as they would say. But, no, that was never the case. By now, it is a matter of survival: with the land cut and mined, the animals gone, immigrants pouring in by the trainload, your people sick and dying.

If this bottle bomb
explodes word scrapnel
flying every which way
responsibility hitting them between the eyes
obligation falling at their feet
justice sticking to their skin
treaty hitting them squarely
and perhaps even a word like suicide
hitting home What would they say?
Would they find the words

I imagine a drum beating, an old drum of worn hide with faint markings of red ocre, the power of another world. The commissioners do not notice this, instead they look at you, your people, and see a life of rags and empty bellies. They complain there are no real Indians left anyway. They say you are merely mimicking something you no longer understand, no longer have words for. There is a moment when they turn to the drummers and wonder when it will all end, wonder when you will finally become Canadians. Not like them, but Canadians nonetheless. In their eyes, you are like children, dependent upon the Queen mother to take care of you.

It gets to the point
where they can no longer ignore me
packing the bomb takes time
my muttering gets to them
but instead of paying attention
to what I'm saying
they run away
and dial 911
say there's a crazy man on his roof
threatening to jump
later they tell me
they did it for my own good.

This is how I see it. From my vantage point, here in this white room, where I sit on top of a mountain of time looking down with the sight of a great eagle. The documents guaranteed health care after plagues were introduced, an education for the children, who were shipped away to residential schools where assimilation was force-fed like the mush they had to eat. But we know this, and we are told there is no use in crying over the past, because the past is today and tomorrow. Past, present and future, a life dipped into and barely held together by an old drum that I can hear even now, way up here on my perch, if I quiet myself and listen hard enough.

Armand Garnet Ruffo

Fish Tale

My father tells me
of catching a northern pike so big
he had to tie a cord to his canoe
and head straight for shore.
And beach the canoe
and haul the beast up
to where he could club it with an axe.
One so big,
he had trouble getting it out
to the road.

He also tells of the time
my mother caught one
and wouldn't give up.
Rolling on the beach,
wrestling fingers to fin,
covered in sand
and slime
trying to stop it from slipping
back into the lake.

He warned her if she kept it
she would carry it herself.
She did.
Slung it over her back
and dragged it a quarter mile.
She had grown up hungry
and this was the biggest fish
she ever caught.
No way
was she going to let it go.

They were young, my parents,
though already with children
they both tried to keep
and lost.
My mother didn't know
the fish could have bit off her hand
or maybe she just didn't care
bent on bringing home food
for the ones left behind.

Armand Garnet Ruffo

Creation Story

Ascending we arrive at the end of the line
descend into Santa Fe, city of my longing
to see the world in a current of silver
and turquoise. Here under a portico of stone
eager tourists press, strangers to the people
who set out their blankets and rows
of jewelry in the age called America.
Here there are boutiques, galleries, churches.
I enter each and arrive to ask, how do we connect
to the sacred space between arrival
and departure? One step
and change is forever.

And I am at another place closer to who I am,
or think I am, steering straight ahead
traveling for what seems like forever,
the sound of waves making me sing its rhythm.
Sixteen and dreaming of offerings of light
in the great beyond. Before I left
and met you, fell out of the sky
of my world, dove overboard,
and came up with a piece of soil
that turned into a warm body who smiled
and said I would never again
be the same.

Santa Fe, city of myth and glitter.
I hold to a company of friends
who hold hands to eyes to shield sun
and talk intimately of love and madness
in a time where power is a slogan,
a bullet, an ability to speak.
What would you say if you could see this stranger
standing in brilliant New Mexico?
This moment an amulet around my neck
I hold and stroke delicately
as though our hands were joined to the years
that amass in the burning heat,
blowing all the way back
to the creation
of us.

Denise Sweet

Song for Discharming

"Hear the voice of my song—it is my voice
        I speak to your naked heart."—Chippewa Charming Song

Before this, I would not do or say what impulse
rushes in to say or do
what instinct burns within
I had learned to temper in my clever sick
while stars unlock at dawn, anonymous as the speed of light
my gray mornings began as nothing, freed of geography
and stripped of any source or consequence.
I was, as you may expect, a human parenthesis.
There is no simple way to say this,
but drift closer, Invisible One, swim within this stream
of catastrophic history. Yours? Mine?
No, you decide. And then

come here one more time so that I may numb like dark
and desperate, so that I may speak your name this final round
you might think an infinite black fog waits to envelope me
you might dream an endless flat of light
you might think I drink
at the very edge of you, cowering like passerine while
hawks hunt the open field of my tiny wars.

but, little by little, like centipedes that whirl and spin
and sink into scorching sands of Sonora
or like gulls at Moningwanekaning that rise and stir
and vanish into the heat lightning of August
I will call you down and bring you into that deathly coil
I will show you each step and stair
I will do nothing and yet it will come to you in this way
That sorcery that swallowed me will swallow you too
At your desired stanza and in a manner of your own making

While I shake the rattle of ferocity moments before sunrise
while I burn sage and sweetgrass, and you, my darling,
while I burn you like some ruined fetish and sing over you
over and over like an almighty voice from the skies
it is in that fragile light
that I will love you
it is in that awakening
I will love myself too
in this dry white drought about to end
in this ghostly city of remember

You will know this, too
and never be able to say.

Moningwanekoning: (Chippewa) Madeline Island, Lake Superior
See migration narratives of Chippewa/Anishinabeeg.

Denise Sweet

Center of Gravity (Antigua, Guatemala, July, 1996)

All things moved from place to place
in the village of San Pedro are balanced
on the head—tubs of tortillas, fold upon
fold of fabric, stiff bundles of firewood,
jugs of water. Women, sometimes children,
walk in grace on narrow sidestreets
sometimes running with an infant slung
at the waist or on their backs—they just go.

No "walk don't walk" signs here to prod
the pedestrian or moments of hesitancy
at crosswalks to cause a tilt in the
center of gravity—they just go:
upright and forward, eyes even
with the horizon, deliberate strides
with a trust that others will see
the difficulty of your burden
and part for you without balking.

You'll not see this amongst the anglos
He whispers, *neither will you see*
The grace among those on foot,
Nor the trust. Mostly the trust.

Maya men carry their bundles in slings
Using an arc to balance the weight
a bend at the waist, the sling anchored
by the head, again the firewood or
textile bundles, sometimes tables and
cabinets from the Mercado
Once a man no taller than me maneuvered
a small black cow through the crowds
a confusion of elbows, hooves and tail
amidst flowered huipiles that day.

179

At eleven I knew about posture and things
too heavy to bear; the sisters of our sacred heart
would lift the chins of small children
demanding straight backs and folded hands
with a single pointed finger, they'd lift
our small bodies over their heads
we'd float over notebooks and catechisms
hovering like small aircraft
waiting to land.

Denise Sweet

Mapping the Land
(*for James Pipe Moustache*)

Like the back of your hand, he said to me,
With one eye a glaucoma gray marble
The brim of his hat shading the good one
*you'll learn the land by feel, each place
a name from memory, each stone
a fingerprint, and the winds:
they have their houses of cedar*

At our feet a five-pound coffee can
of spit and chew; the old man leans towards it
and with remarkable aim, deposits the
thin brown liquid without missing a
step *I never thought much of the running,
the miles between home and
Tomah boarding school* he has since
teased me about the relays
the long-distance marathons, the logic of
treadmills. Who could explain that to this old man?

The sport of running with no destination
no purpose, slogging like wild-eyed sundancers
foolish in the heat, snapping at gnats
and no-seeums, signifying sovereignty
step by step on two-lane highways
raising the dust in unincorporated redneck towns
fluorescent Nikes kicking up blacktop
ogitchiidaa carrying the eagle staff
like an Olympian torch.

Back then we packed hard the trails
banking it for those with no shoes
schoolchildren, none older than nine or ten
wise in their running—a month or two and then
they would be rounded up like calves into
wagons; Indian agents once again
emptying the villages of their young

the older ones who spoke no English
slipped into their own shadows, kept still
in beds of bulrushes familiar and safe,
holding their breath as winter constellations
set compass, as northern lights danced
in a whir overhead, keeping track in
old-time ways of knowing.

Home in a week by sundown, he grinned,
Every time. They'd never catch us
his cupped hands resting on an ironwood cane,
peyote stitched at the crook by his niece
the old man looks straight ahead and then to me
But I never finished the seventh grade, my girl
The sudden twist of regret hung in the air
between us: I hardly knew what to say,
whether ignorance or stamina should be
his disgrace, whether I could have found
my way back home, lost within the
indecipherable space of the *chiimokomon*

Denise Sweet

And would I run again and again to return
where education and bleak seasons of absence
would come within the harvest of stories
Or, like some, would I have learned
the hard way: blinded by light
Frozen in terror like a rabbit, faking death
To stay alive?

ogitchiidaa: mediating force; warrior
chiimokomon: non-Indian; predominant culture

Zen and Woman's Way of Parking

We know sooner than we think
when the vehicle we are driving
refuses to be herded into its stall.
We crank the wheel and ease our way
around and in and back and forth
and then back out and forward and in
again and then back and forth and
back and forth 'til we have neatly
and carefully negotiated a big thing
into a small space. "It's all in the
wrist" when we speak of power steering
or, for that matter, our lover. And yet,

it is a maneuver that requires integration
of our body, mind, and spirit. The contortive
efforts of the driver imitate Hatha yoga
positionings, as we are expected to see
front and behind, this side and that side
all at the same time. Be in the here and now
in the parking lot. Serenity is not far behind.
Neither is the Volvo parked in the next lane.

And how quickly we computate space, density,
width, length and probability at that moment we
grind the gears from first to reverse and back
again; after careful deliberation, the geniuses
that we are, we arrive at the parking nudge
principle: simply put, it is necessary and
a tender act to nudge the vehicle to the front
and back of us as we locate parameters of the
space we are to become. Oh to be parked in a
stall of our own, but spiritually connected with
all that exists around us. Nirvana is achieved.

Denise Sweet

And the headlights are on.

Let them call us "ladydrivers" let them curse
and shake their fists at "the battle axe behind
the wheel." We'll give them no fast break,
no free ride; indeed we will not yield
even though the sign insists. Oh sisters,
this is the right of way revolution,
a woman's way of parking is knowing and seeing
and feeling our way around this hard, flat
landscape we call parking space. We have finally
come to a place of which we surely belong.
We are at last in the driver's seat,
and we laugh in the face of cruise control.

Red Dogs in the Heat (Taos Pueblo, 1996)

All day long in the name of commerce
and Taoan hospitality, the gates of the
pueblo stay open; tourists move from
table to table speculating on rain
and uptown prices at Indian Market
Vendors and their grandchildren
stack pow wow tapes and refold t-shirts
papago baskets and pots from Acoma
sit like roosting hens under the ramada

A man in madras shorts stirs through
a tray of fetishes, carved coral and
pale turquoise from Pauite territory.
He raises a jukala necklace
like a rattlesnake from its nest
asking his wife, *Do you think this is real?*

The woman shrugs, touches her hair
in the absence of mirrors or scarves.
Cicadas whirl like tiny firecrackers
lit by the heat and glare of all
that silver waiting in clusters to be chosen.
The vendor who will speak only in Tewa
to her grandson, continues to string
beads, scooping them from a small plate
with her long thin needle. Neither speaks
much.

Suddenly a dog, a pueblo mixed blood
belonging to no one in the village
raises an issue with his cousins
the scurrying pack divides
the nervous crowd at once
the older dogs twist and torment
themselves in the heat, aiming
to keep turf at any cost

Denise Sweet

Two old Taoan men sit and chuckle
in their lawn chairs, sipping diet cokes,
their chins jutting towards the ruckus,
A student with the tour group
snaps a photo of the old woman shaking
a switch at the disturbance, sending dogs
in all directions. The instigator snaps
at his own shadow, and collapses in the
shade under someone's porch. He'll
settle it later.

Not everyone moves comfortably after this
the tour guide points toward Blue Lake
and the centuries-old pueblo structure
a visitor asks for bottled water
and a clean toilet   another asks
for a website address, and like a
well-rehearsed battalion, the group
disperses to board the bus humming
with cool air and adjustable seats.
Brown-faced and sweating, children
wave at the visitors in the dust
waving until the bus
is well out of sight.

Art does not come easy, Tony
remarks, molding micaceous clay with
thick brown fingers   he calls me
young lady   we sit in the cool
of his adobe studio
gray moths collect on the screen door
I'd managed my way to stay
inside Taos after dark, the ground
still radiating heat through my sandals

The fire packed within the ground
will smolder for days, blue-white heat
building within the vessels—any weakness
or hairline crack, and the eccentric one
will explode, angered by reckless
impatience, destroying the whole batch

Keepers of the Fire, you are relatives
of this village, of this mountain
runners in the heat
Earth Water Fire
Earth Water Fire
Tony grins and hands
over a smooth stone
for polishing green clay,
he directs my hands
in slow circles of the shoulders
of each pot.

At 77, he still runs at dawn, carrying
corn pollen along the small stream,
trailed by dogs of the village on
a path older than the buildings
they run mornings to keep ahead
of the heat or the tourists or
maybe to test for cracks
tectonic weaknesses in the
foothills of Sierra Madre

Grandfather of clay
of blue water,
of volcanic fires,
the children of the well
are still running.

We are still running.

Denise Sweet

Indian War

It's hard enough to make simple talk of this
Watching turkey feathers and greasepaint grins
Dance akimbo upon the TV screen,
The painted quarterhorses carrying costumed
(b)raves, the rider screaming as though aflame.
I'm disgusted by what I would like to say—
The hurtful words I learned from punks—
None will fit neatly into the fatness of gratitude
You're expecting to hear from your Indians
The ones you honor at half-time.

The parallels to Stepin Fetchit escape you
Though you know as well as I do
That the "N" word will never show up
On a football jersey—
your eyes go blank when I tell you
our skin turned red only when it
was treated like bounty, human flesh
torn from muscle and bone,
the trade worth less than beaver pelts
You have no memory of this
And I cannot forget it.

I could say eagle headdresses and
catholic chalices, talk about religious
freedom and name the 730 Ghost Dancers
shot down in America's first Waco
admit the hideous self-loathing that sweeps
through our children like political smallpox
but it is no good; my throat is parched
my voice ragged and I disgrace
my grandfather with all this
unnecessary begging.

On the prairie of justice and imagination
I go back to the lakotah nation and
The tradition of restraint and male mockery,
Making war by making a point
Where a warrior would steer
His swift horse directly towards
An enemy close enough to
Thwack the adams apple
Close enough to smear feces
in his hair, close enough to
Slap his cheek and ride away
in lowbelly laughter
and send that soldier
back to his troops
Limping with shame.

Listen: I'm calling out to the 500 nations
That reside on this continent
Those like me who want more than this
Those who want to roll back
the Astroturf like Wovoka described,
to coax the yellow undergrowth
back into waves of prairie grass
we'll watch the goodyear blimp
combast with grandeur over
Paha Sapa, listening for the thunders
To give the last 10-minute warning:
time enough to learn about the end
of the world and time enough
to finally learn of playing fair.

Mark Turcotte

Gravity

Back when I used to be Indian
I am counting the stars
in the night of my mother's eyes.
Five, four, three.
Her husband is heaped in the corner,
chains rattling in his throat.
She groans and lifts herself
finally from the floor. A bone explodes
in her neck. She begins to spin.
Two, one.
The darkness pulls me.
Another glowing cinder drops
out of the sky.

Visitation

Back when I used to be Indian
I am six maybe seven
years old, restless, pretending to sleep
in the dry glow of the cast-iron
stove. My sister's back is warm
and still against my own.
A straw in the blanket scratches my ankle.
Somewhere in the darkness
my mother and her husband grunt
and hiss, hands over mouths.
I blink.
Across the room a buffalo snorts,
nudges the yellow Tonka truck
with its nose.

Mark Turcotte

Flies Buzzing

Somewhere in america, in a certain state of grace . . .
Patti Smith

As a child I danced
to the heartful, savage
rhythm
of the Native, the
American Indian,
in the Turtle Mountains,
in the Round Hall,
in the greasy light of
kerosene lamps.

As a child I danced
among the long, jangle legs of
the men, down
    beside the whispering moccasin women,
in close circles
around the Old Ones,
who sat at the drum,
their heads tossed, backs arched
    in ancient prayer.

As a child I danced away from the fist,
I danced toward the rhythm of life,
I danced into dreams, into
    the sound of flies buzzing.
A deer advancing but clinging to the forest wall,
the old red woman rocking in her tattered shawl,
the young women bent, breasts
drooping to the mouths of their young, the heat
hanging heavy on the tips of our tongues,
until the Sun
burned the sky black, the moon
made us silvery blue and
all of the night sounds, all of the night sounds

folded together with the buzzing
still in our heads,
becoming a chant of ghosts,
of *Crazy Horse* and *Wovoka*
and all the endless Others
snaking through the weaving through the trees
like beams of ribbons of light
    singing, *we shall live again we shall live,*

until the Sun and the Sun and the Sun and I
awaken,
still a child, still dancing
toward the rhythm of life.

Mark Turcotte

Cyrus Calls For His Pony

When they buried you, Cyrus,
I was ashamed
of the casket and the lid,
knowing how you dreamed
of a breathing cradle of moss and ferns,

knowing that you grumbled
and staggered to Mass
under the heat
of your crooked suit,
only to make your woman happy.

Returning, you would dust
off your sleeves, twist your hands,
wink at us boys,
point your chin to the woods
and whisper,
    it's out there, in the trees.

Cyrus, how simply deeply
you remain with me.
Even now I smile
when I remember the last time
I saw you,

so old, so curled up
by your bones.

You pointed with your chin
to where your battered walker
leaned in the corner
and whispered,
    bring me my pony, boy, I gotta pee.

Hands

Old man,
I stood over you in your box,
and when I reached to touch your gray folded hands,
I remembered, suddenly, a fair summer day beside big water,
when you laughed and lifted me
higher than the trees,

and I felt like a big boy,
I felt like a big boy,
in your hands I felt like a good boy,
and you said,
    hey Chee-pwa,
    do you see any angels up there, do you see any angels?

Old man,
I leaned over you in your box,
touched my hands into your thin gray wave of hair,
and I whispered,
    may the Grandfathers give you feathers, all is forgiven down here . . .

Doyle Turner, Jr.

Siren

What is description, after all, but encoded desire?
—Mark Doty

You, too, own a swamp
gaseous and rotting
a constant gurgle percolating

deep pots entangled
in vessel, sinew, and bone
an acid that could preserve

a man for decades.
A mirror for the seasons
sometimes it resembles

a lake, the feathery
fineness of the auburn
tamarack gathering wind.

There is something that
lives there, reaches for
your feet as you pass,

you roll down your window
finger the scent, a
candy lined up

along the path
passing this place
almost daily now.

You can skip along
the surface, hit the
hollowed pit

of a wave, the gate
pressing sound from your ears
bubbled yells would only

burp like any other
escaping "plop." Silt like
china, breakable with a

wave of the hand
now holding your shoulders
"no one will know, no

one will find you" no
terror only a sediment
settling sure in your

chest.

Doyle Turner, Jr.

Waiting for Fish

It seemed like a moment of sun,
that day interrupted by water,
so perfect in the afternoon sun,
water,
a promise of spring,
dead reeds along its banks.

Water
flowing, washing away the
ice of another winter
feeding the culvert we stood upon.
Dad telling stories of old Indian
men, our relatives,
pushing out logs from the river's edge,
standing on the ends like
cranes,
Ajijaak, spearing fish on springtime
days during the northern spawn.

Fish longer
than your arms could spread wide,
as long as this much, not so long ago.
Stories, stealing enough truth to test
your willingness to believe.
Ripples of fish
crossing the river
up stream.
Fins as big as your hands
waving to you from the boggy banks,
sneak up as they splash
watch where your shadow falls
hold
still. We saw small fat northerns glide in
and out of the culvert.

Doyle Turner, Jr.

Father and son watched as the truck idled,
a reminder of watery time passing through
our lives, the culverts.
Our hands missing the
half-wet handle
of our spring spears.

Doyle Turner, Jr.

The Filling Station Treatment

"Warmer weather's movin in,"
but by the time you mention
that you've driven through
soggy flakes
of late spring cold,
hypnotizing and
mesmerizing you
like railroad cars
numbering by
at the crossing
of a misplaced
small town,
he's already
run his eyes
across your wife through
the sky-tinted windows
he's off
to check the oil.

When you ask
"Where are the restrooms?"
he hesitates and squints at you
as if you are the one
who has been leaving the toilet plugged
for the last 16 years.

And as you pay
$1.94 for two cans of pop
and say to "have a good day"
he's looking past you
at the prairie clouds
rolling in
like another high-tide,
probably thinking about
the cars it will wave
through town,
through his station,
coming again to
leave him behind.

Turtle Heart

broken pots

(in memory of two elders now passed over)

old red-skins
polished like old sacred drums
skins that move through time
dreaming ahead
and behind their ancient shadow
walking in our sleep
we might have danced with them
awake at last
we can eat their spirits like corn
left behind
upon a shrinking path
i sent a song into the mountain
and made it wet, the rain marking my fingers
with the silence of the waiting world
where I sat inside myself
remembering everything
broken pots scattered before me like a shouting into the wind

dream stone

black ravens
eat the hearts of turtles
in the desert
they drop them on the stones
from up in the sky
and sleep in the trash at the edge of town
dreaming
i found myself on my belly
whispering a song to the earth
pressed into a flat rock
my old clothes made of hair
outside the light was blowing around
blowing with the wild wind
i could hear old feet dancing out there
dancing in the golden dust
when i went outside
i found a blue stone
where his toes had been
i tied it to a raven's black feather

i wear it in my hair
when i go to town

on the way to the house of dreamers

i have gone walking on the earth
i look with two hands at what is before me
i was the one who was there
i was the one digging up my own life
from the scattered dust of time
i took with two hands
what was before me
it was right there on the earth
that is where the mystery life had placed it

right there
on the ground
i have taken it

tree singing (sacred pipes)

someone said they could go
into the earth
and sit there singing
some have said they would go
up into trees
standing stone people
were the ones who sent them there
sitting high up in the trees
trees grown from the sacred roots
where they were one day
sitting inside the earth and singing
with those stones. . . .

E. Donald Two-Rivers

Rebels With a Bottom Line Consciousness

They put a Starbucks right there on Wilson Avenue
Where the bad boys laid and played
Back in the day.
Right up the street from Blood Alley
Where I slap boxed and body punched my way to respectability
They installed a Starbucks and what, I wondered,
would that mean to the boys?
I hear Men's Wear is interested in the strip too.
And Banana Republic . . . maybe a Cub Foods.
Investment opportunities is the buzz.
Put in a store with a big burly 'yes Maam' security guard
To keep the boys moving . . .
Hire a thug to protect those looking
for bohemia without the bohemians
Keep the boys moving and out of sight.
Gentrification, the new removal policy,
bulls its way into the hood
and suddenly life long residents are problem people . . .
a perspective that some local politicians can be sold . . .
Keep the boys moving and out of sight.
Gentrification follows the artist community . . .
That weird but pretty façade
That masks the whole thing
They whisper that it is too profitable
To question consequences or impacts.
Rebels with a bottom line consciousness
Smiling one day and dancing away the next.

E. Donald Two-Rivers

"They recast their role to become
entrepreneurs in a cultural marketplace."
The thing is about business, but I have memories
of Wilson Avenue that won't fade away.
my memories are of Southern belles
with sugared accents and lustful thoughts.
Oh how we mixed up those races back in the day
and we had the balls
to believe we could elect an alderman.
my memories are of Indian boys struttin on Wilson
charming in head-bands and chokers
and Island folks with visions of drums
and water and sand and bared flesh
visions warmed by the sun.
blacks coming on buses to
live in Urban Renewals' big deception.

keep the boys moving cause their day is done!
keep the boys moving let them dream on the run.

longtime locals are problem people
victimized by entrepreneurs who short change reality
with lip service political correctness.
like bohemians with shades and trench coats . . .
babbling ad copy and sanitizing hunger.
A market ploy, a whitewashed image . . .
the Golden Rule stylized for profit . . .
a lesser sin dancing past the Taj Mahal
like an obedient servant in Banana Republic underwear.

a young woman gyrates on a street corner hoping for a better day.
A preacher removes his collar, parks his Cadillac
and asks "how much?"
She looks at him and chants, "life is hectic   distractions are expensive
sort of like a future plan for eighth grade drop-out."
"space is the place," he answered, "where life produces sexual acts that
make a difference."
she tilted her head, rubbed her thighs together and asked
if he was circumcised.
That was a huge piece of information
he wouldn't divulge.
he crossed himself and walked away
to a national Cuff Links Society exhibit
of old man Bush's cuff links . . .
Like an annual endeavor . . .
At its very best: thought provoking
                    You're the good thing.
                 Like food, music or drink
                 so let's create good karma!
                    Let's create love!
            Let's create a story where everyone lives in peace,
                 including the bottom-line rebels.

E. Donald Two-Rivers

Rambo to Flambeau

Spirits of northern lakes
churned in anger
as PARR people wrapped in flags
and singing songs of hate
entered a new day of racism
at Wisconsin landing sites.

A lynch mob of Amerikans—
high strung in Kodiak boots,
plaid shirts and shot guns—
ride dangerous and deadly
in pickup trucks.
Souls of hate glisten like silver gun racks
in war wagons with bumper stickers that say
"save a deer, shoot an Indian."

Blood stains chrome,
dancing flames glare
in Wisconsin's nights.
The metaphysics of racism
is based on real estate aspirations
of the powers that are.
Who, though, made one race the classifiers?
Who decides how to categorize us
or to tuck comfortably away
those images that no longer sell?
Who so arrogantly believes
they can divide us all like that
Our sons and daughters of every generation
seek to love and yet arguments float about
and we're divided
into national spheres of colonization.

"Rambo to Flambeau!" they shout
with weapons held at "ready, aim, fire!"
The issue is hardly about walleyes.

Always scared
all the way to the bone
and even to the marrow
the hate-filled messages sound menacing.
Tension squeezes in alongside the fear
and ignorance is pure
and sung in a raspy voice
that grates on the mean souls.

Bleeding flames of hate
from sky blue eyes,
they scream in protest against treaties
they don't understand,
victims of a deleted history
that's been stripped of truth.

They scream in the night.
"Rambo to Flambeau! Rambo to Flambeau!"

Everyone is a product of environments.
Wrong perceptions dance,
and those old Indian images.
pressed into hereditary memory,
jump out at you in full color,
through words like "savage,"
"murder," "revenge," "heathens."
Anthropological misconceptions.

E. Donald Two-Rivers

With spatulas of deception
they stir fires of distrust.
Brewing a formula of racial
and economic insecurity
they spread fear and hate rumors
based on outright lies
that flutter about in northern winds
like fallen leaves
that stick to hunter's boots on rainy days.
Collected experience through words
Like "savage," "murder," "revenge," "heathens."

"Rambo to Flambeau! Rambo to Flambeau!"
they scream and wave flags
with weapons held at "Ready, aim, fire!"
The issue is hardly about walleyes
The intent anything but honorable.

Flags waving, they scream
"Rambo to Flambeau! Rambo to Flambeau!"

Not on the Guest List
For Dennis Banks of AIM

Oh, but could we partake
of the democratic process
our ancestors gifted to them.
Someone slammed the door
on our ghetto world.
We're not on the guest list,
and resolution 204
sits hidden away deeper even than
the "license for sale" scam.
Now their arrogance
has been slung around our lives.
Now we're jumping through hoops
hoping for a measure of dignity.

We're fighting in a silent class war.
With a twist of the head they glance at us
then look away like we're unlisted numbers.
Chief Illinowick is the governor's hero.
"It's an honorable thing.
It's an honorable thing!!"
says the dishonorable bastard.
204! 204! 204! Don't lose sight of 204.
The hocus pocus is straight-armed to the side.

Is history about to be repeated?
Is Annie Oakley there
on the 9th floor at Clark and Randolph?
Who is that woman trying
to act like an Indian agent
with a loaf of bread,
a brick of commodity cheese,
a broken old concept of a treaty,
and a request for a powwow?
She comes off like a Prozac queen.

E, Donald Two Rivers

We came looking for solutions
with suggestions and good will we came.
Is it an annoyance when we ask for respect?
And now you are talking at us like
we are your personal Tonto's
in Hollywood buckskin. Slow down, Kemosabe!
It's dignity we came to talk about.
You were going to fulfill
House Resolution 204. That's the issue.
Not a powwow at State and Lake.

We are those sovereign savages
who won't buy your hype—
no seamless assimilation.
And NO GREAT WHITE FATHER.
No step-and-fetch can replace mutual respect.
Looking around seeing
the brown, black, and white faces
of other uninvited guests,
we see a look of recognition.
A silent message is passed with a nod or smile.
A closed fist to the heart
and our mutual experience is there,
bared and visible and a threat.
We all know something has got to change.
Let us make it be the removal of distrust
based on the color of our skin.
We're not on the guest list not any of us.

Oh but could we partake of the democratic
process that our ancestors gifted to them.

Gerald Vizenor

Family Photograph

among trees
my father was a spruce

corded for tribal pulp
he left the white earth reservation
colonial genealogies
taking up the city at twenty-three

telling stories
sharing dreams from a mason jar
running
low through the stumps at night
was his line

at twenty-three
he waited with the old men
colorless
dressed in their last uniforms
reeling on the nicollet island bridge

arm bands adrift
wooden limbs
men too civilized by war
thrown back to evangelists and charity

no reservation superintendents there
no indian agents
pacing off allotments twenty acres short
only family photographs ashore

no catholics on the wire
tying treaty money to confirmations

Gerald Vizenor

in the city
my father was an immigrant
hanging paper flowers
painting ceilings white for a union boss
disguising saint louis park

his weekend women
listened to him measuring my blood at night

downtown rooms were cold
half truths
peeling like blisters of history
two sizes too small

he smiles
holding me in a photograph then
the new spruce
half white
half immigrant
taking up the city and losing at cards

Seven Woodland Crows

seven woodland crows
stayed all winter
this year
among the white earth trees

down around us on the edge of roads
passing in the eyes of strangers
tribal land wire marked
fox runs under rusting plows

stumps for eagles

white winter savages
with brackish blue eyes
snaring their limbs on barbed wire

brackish winter blood

seven woodland crows
stayed all winter
this year
marking the dead
landmen who ran the woodland
out of breath

fat green flies
square dance across the grapefruit
honor your partner

hail stones
sound once or twice a summer
old school bell

Gerald Vizenor

plum blossoms
burst in a sudden storm
faces in a pool

Natural Duty

high flowers
planted in the spring
a natural duty
to the hummingbirds
already conceals
a black cat

every shadow
an eternal tease
of creation
floral dominion
over flight
strays alone
by late afternoon

Gerald Vizenor

Jeweler

mystic words
shudder
on the glass
ancient names
plundered

memories
afire overnight
on the train
antwerp
to amsterdam

old shadows
almost lost
by utter war
lighten
hand and stone

slight tributes
only agony
crease my face
on the cold
cloudy window

bright traces
beholden
to a jeweler
evermore
blest in motion

Almost Ashore

winter sea
over my shoes
shadow
last stones

every wave
turns a season
underfoot
memory of fire

tidal pools
slight my hand
shoulders
almost ashore

light breaks
my traces
blood, bone, stone
natural seams

photograph by Vance Vannote

Kimberly Blaeser, Editor

Kimberly Blaeser is a Professor of English at the University of Wisconsin-Milwaukee where she teaches courses in Native American Literature, Creative Writing, and American Nature Writing. An enrolled member of the Minnesota Chippewa Tribe, she grew up on the White Earth Reservation. Blaeser's publications include two collections of poetry, *Trailing You,* which won the 1993 First Book Award from the Native Writers Circle of the Americas, and *Absentee Indians and Other Poems* (2002). She is also the author of a critical study, *Gerald Vizenor: Writing in the Oral Tradition,* and the editor of a collection of Anishinaabe prose, *Stories Migrating Home.* Her poetry, short fiction, personal essays, introductions, and scholarly articles have been published in more than forty Canadian and American collections including *Earth Song, Sky Spirit, Reinventing the Enemy's Language, Narrative Chance, Women on Hunting, The Colour of Resistance, This Giving Birth, Dreaming History, As We Are Now, Returning the Gift, Talking on the Page, Other Sisterhoods, Unsettling America, Skins, Sister Nations, Nothing But the Truth, After Confession,* and *Blue Dawn, Red Earth.* One of Blaeser's poems was selected for installation as a sculptured doorway in the Midwest Express Building in Milwaukee. She has lectured or read from her work in over 100 locations in the United States, Canada, and Europe, had one of her talks chosen by Writers' Conferences and Festivals for inclusion in the organization's anthology of the best lectures given in 1992, and was chosen to inaugurate the Western Canada Lecture Series in 1995. Blaeser was recipient of a

Wisconsin Arts Board fellowship in poetry in 2001 and the winner of a Writer of the Year Award from Wordcraft Circle of Native Writers in 2003 for a personal essay. Currently at work on a creative collage, *Family Tree*, she lives with her husband and two young children in the woods and wetlands of rural Lyons Township, Wisconsin.

❦

Twin energies—need and pleasure—have always driven my writing. As a shy child, I often used imagination and, when I was old enough, writing as a personal survival tool. Later the desire grew to carry the memories and stories of family, tribe, and community into a colonized world that had over and over proved itself hostile to our histories and beliefs, that had many times worked to possess even the literary traditions of Native peoples. I work to honor these Indigenous literatures through my teaching, writing, and publishing.

Entwined with this determination was fascination and simple delight in language. Poetry, for example, depends deeply upon the heard elements of the spoken, upon the music of voice, the rhythms of sound, spaces, accents. My love for these soundings of language came partly from the habit of the oral, my life within a family that performed story as an everyday act. Both sides of my immediate and my extended families at White Earth are filled with talented and colorful storytellers. I grew up amid people who not only made of the everyday incidents lively accounts, but who sang, recited, teased, imitated, read out loud—whose entertainment was often joyful verbal exchanges. The love of language is in many ways a gift we inherit.

My own writing draws on many sources for inspiration including encounters with the natural world, the experiences of motherhood, my Native heritage, the complications of all our loves, the work of fellow writers, and the oxymoron of justice politics. I am ever a student of writing, working just now with the haiku tradition, exploring the dynamics of collage, and continuing a series of poems informed by my family histories. Words are my singular intoxication.

Joe Geshick, cover artist

Ojibway artist Joe Geshick's paintings of traditional Indian ceremonies represent a kind of personal thanksgiving. Their clear, integral designs and richly textured layers of vibrant earth tones express a sense of calmness and simplicity, hidden strength and deep spiritual connection with the natural world. Joe's artwork reflects the healing power of these ceremonies and extend his gratitude for their impact on his life.

Born on June 21, 1943 near Faribault, Minnesota, Joe began painting at 19. In the late 70s, he studied at the Art Students League in New York. While attending school, he worked at the Museum of the American Indian, where he made pen and ink drawings of the museum artifacts. After completing his studies in New York, Joe moved to the Lac La Croix reserve in Ontario, Canada, where he taught art in an elementary school. From Canada, Joe moved to Reno, Nevada, where he taught art and eventually established his own art studio.

During his stay in Lac La Croix, Joe learned the history of his clan, discovered his Ojibway name, Mishakeebaneesh, and was introduced to traditional ceremonies. In 1977, for the first time, Joe participated in the annual Sundance Ceremony at Greengrass, South Dakota. Through five years of sundancing, Joe's spiritual development became firmly rooted in the traditional ceremonies, bringing a new understanding into his life.

The deepening influence of this involvement in traditional ceremonies also brought about a change in his work as an artist. Shifting away from his prior concentration on landscapes, still lifes, portraits, and seascapes, Joe began experimenting with the palette knife to paint traditional images drawn from his experiences with the ceremonies, using the six sacred colors—red, yellow, black, white, green and blue. Out of respect to the sacred nature of ceremonial objects such as pipes and medicine bundles, Joe chooses not to use such images in his work.

Of his painting, *The Spirit Helper*, he says "it is my version of a medicine man seeking help from his spirit helpers."

kateri akiwenzie-damm

I am an Anishnaabe writer of mixed ancestry from the Chippewas of Nawash First Nation. I live and work at Neyaashiinigmiing, Cape Croker Reserve on the Saugeen Peninsula in southwestern Ontario. My writing has been published in a collection, *my heart is a stray bullet;* a chapbook, *bloodriver woman*; and various anthologies, journals and magazines in Canada, the U.S., Aotearoa/New Zealand, Australia, and Germany. I guest edited a special issue of *Rampike* Literary and Arts magazine (an issue featuring the work of Indigenous writers); and am the co-editor of *skins: contemporary Indigenous writing*, an international anthology of fiction by Indigenous writers co-published by Kegedonce Press and Aboriginal Australian publisher, Jukurrpa Books. Both of these collections were released in the fall of 2000. In 2001, I served on the National Caucus of the Wordcraft Circle of Native Writers and Storytellers. In February 2003 "Beneath the Buffalo Robe," a radio piece co-written and performed with Gregory Scofield, aired nationally on CBC Radio One. *Without Reservation*, an anthology of erotica by Indigenous writers, which I compiled and edited, was released in Canada and Aotearoa in the autumn of 2003. I was a librettist with composer Timothy Sullivan on a composition for the Bell'Arte Singers, a 50-voice choir in Toronto, which premiered October 18, 2003 and is slated for more performances in 2004. For the past two years I spearheaded "Honouring Words: International Indigenous Authors Celebration Tour" and coordinated the inaugural international tour in Canada in October 2002. *standing ground*, a CD of my spoken word poetry with music by Indigenous collaborators from Aotearoa, Canada, the U.S., and South America, was released in March 2004 and has been featured on local and national radio in Canada. Currently I have a grant to complete a collection of short stories. I am also completing a collection of poetry, various publishing projects and am working on a multidisciplinary multimedia piece with acclaimed choreographer Santee Smith and award winning hip-hop artist Te Kupu.

My work is a way of attempting to express beauty, truth, and love. It is a way of connecting with those around me, of sharing what I am learning, of saying what I cannot speak, of praying. For me, writing is ceremony. Words are powerful. They can change the world. I write as an Anishnaabekwe, a woman of mixed ancestry from the Chippewas of Nawash First Nation. I write to tell something of who we are, to know myself, to remember, to celebrate life, to transform the injustice and hatred and lovelessness around me into something creative and positive. I am inspired by the land, by my ancestors, by the friends and lovers and enemies who have been my teachers. My work is influenced by a literary tradition of songs, stories, chants, prayers, invocations, and oratories from the Anishnaabek people as well as others around me. I give love and thanks to my community, my family, the web of Indigenous writers, orators and storytellers that stretches around me, and especially to those who share my life with all of its laughter and despair and teach me what I need to know. To the ones I love and to those before and after: chi meegwetch. K'zaugin.

David Beaulieu

David Beaulieu is the director of the Center for Indian Education at Arizona State University. The former University of Wisconsin-Milwaukee School of Education's first Electa Quinney endowed professor of American Indian Education, he is an enrolled member of the Minnesota Chippewa Tribe from White Earth Reservation. Beaulieu served as the director of the U.S. Department of Education's Office of Indian Education from 1997 to 2002. Previously, he served as Commissioner of the Minnesota Department of Human Rights, the first American Indian to be appointed to such a post in state government. He also served on the Indian Nations at Risk Task Force. Dr. Beaulieu has teaching and/or administrative experience at several institutions including the University of Minnesota; Sinte Gleska College in Rosebud, South Dakota, where he served as Vice President; and the Minnesota Department of Education where he served as State Director of Indian Education. He is a member of the Board of Directors and President Elect of the National Indian Education Association and member of the Board and Secretary for the National Trust for Excellence in Native American Education established by the United States Congress. His research interests are broadly related to the education of the American Indian. Dr. Beaulieu earned his Master's and his Ph.D. in Education Administration from the University of Minnesota.

"Lost Memories" and an earlier work "Crows'" published by Loonfeather Press in *Stories Migrating Home: A Collection of Anishinaabe Prose* are part of a larger narrative "The Strange Empire of John Clement Beaupre." I began writing John Clement stories nearly ten years ago and have added to them usually through periods of significant personal change. The stories are personal reflections and reflections of other men I have known which have combined somehow in my imagination into the character of John Clement Beaupre. When I began, I considered the traditional Anishinaabe Winnebosho narrative and realized that these stories must have been invented by someone, by the first storyteller, I suppose, and I also realized that new stories were constantly being invented to reflect significant changes in contemporary Ojibwe life such as Winnebosho and the game warden. Someone is constantly adding to this grand collection; it is remembered and told over and over again. I also remember groups of Ojibwe men telling stories about each other, usually creating a character with a particular name that often referred to one in the group. These were usually funny, made all the more so by the fact that they usually referred to someone in the group who most often was present. The style of these stories was like the more funny Winnebosho stories such as skunk power. Many of these stories were invented on the spot and were hilarious. As a storyteller, the character John Clement Beaupre is for me an invention, an alter ego I suppose, told in a style which is reminiscent of an Anishinaabe way of telling stories.

Alice Bird

I grew up on the Black River Reservation and my life has been a simple one filled with family and friends. My half-century has seen a lot of changes for my community and has offered me experiences as varied as the modes of transportation that cover the distance between the natural wilderness and so-called civilization. These differences and the ways they play off each other give shades of meaning to my vivid memories. I've lived my life to the fullest in my roles as daughter, sister, wife, mother, grandmother, and elder. I have walked both roads.

I returned to school to accomplish two main goals: first and most importantly, to lay down a path for my children and grandchildren to follow; secondly, to stretch myself and grow intellectually as a way of expressing my spiritual self.

I write because I have to. The images and memories from my past are as alive to me as the world around us.

Shirley Brozzo

I am Anishnaabe and a member of the Keweenaw Bay Tribe of Chippewa Indians. Having been born and raised in Ironwood, Michigan, then moving to Marquette in 1989 makes me a lifelong Yooper! For many years I have been employed by Northern Michigan University as their GAP Coordinator. GAP is a retention program for academically and economically disadvantaged students, which translates to working mainly with students of color. I am currently serving as the Assistant Director of Diversity Student Services and as an Adjunct Instructor for the Center for Native American Studies at Northern Michagan University.

In 1992 I earned my Bachelor's degree in business administration and in 1994 a Master of Arts in English, both at NMU. I am currently pursuing a Master of Fine Arts (MFA) also at NMU. Since 1995 I have been in the classroom as an adjunct instructor for the Center for Native American Studies.

I have three adult children, Jamie, Brandi and Steven. My current hobbies include working puzzles, reading, and crocheting.

I am inspired by the world around me. By this I mean I listen to words and phrases that people say and create images to respond to what I hear. Also, I see injustices that are done, funny things that happen, a smile from a dear friend, and I am moved to write. I know that there is at least one female spirit who watches over me when I write or embark on an adventure. She helps me in untold ways. All of my life experiences blend together to create scenarios for me to write about. I draw from good times and bad, my children by birth as well as those who choose to call me "mom," and reactions to things I see or read. Anything I encounter could possibly show up again in my writings, and often does!

Ardie Medina Buckholtz

Ardie Medeina Buckholtz, Anishinaabe from the Lac du Flambeau Indian Reservation in northern Wisconsin, began writing poetry when she was 13 years old. Since moving to Minneapolis in 1993, she has expanded into prose, short stories and writing plays.

Twice a participant in The Loft Literary Center's Native American In-Roads program under the mentorships of Heid Erdrich and Diane Glancy, Ardie was also a member of The Playwright Center's Native American Roundtable under the mentorship of Marcie Rendon.

For three summers Ardie participated in The Minnesota Fringe Festival as both writer and actor (*Rites of Passage, Stolen Generation* and *Back to the Blanket*) and actor (*The Free Frybread Telethon* which premiered at Bryant Lake Bowl and also went on the road to perform at the Turtle Lake Casino in Turtle Lake, Wisconsin).

Ardie has also been involved in several productions of the Twin Cities Women's Choir and SASE: The Write Place. Through her work with these two organizations, Ardie was one of five poets commissioned by the Weisman Art Museum to write poems based on the Museum's New Voices of the Heartland exhibit in 2002. She was also commissioned to write poetry for the Twin Cities Women's Choir's spring concert in 2003 entitled *Strong Hearts Leading the Way*, a performance piece of music and spoken word.

She is currently serving as Development Director for The Loft Literary Center in Minneapolis.

Poetry has always been a way for me to go beyond what my eyes see, to go into my very soul to gauge how it is reacting. I am not particularly methodical or disciplined about my writing. But I find when I really have something to say, when I really want to be heard, my creativity and words rarely abandon me.

All things inspire me to write—memories, feelings, a smell, a sound, images—anything. Life, in general, moves me to create. I strive not to create a mystery with my words, but to paint a path that the reader can easily follow—go where I am, whether in truth or imaginings. So he or she can say, "I've been here—I know this."

Pauline Danforth

I was born in Minneapolis, Minnesota but spent my childhood in Pine Point, a tiny community on the White Earth Reservation. Here I felt prairie and woodland winds, listened to my grandmother and the older women gossip and tell stories, and observed the Catholic and Midewiwin rituals swirl around me. Fast forward to the present. I recently completed my Ph.D. in American Studies, am raising my seven-year-old son adopted from my extended family, and am working for TRIO/Student Support Services at Metropolitan State University in retaining students underrepresented in higher education. In my free time I write poetry, short stories, and book reviews that echo the sage wisdom of my childhood and the continuity of my reservation-urban experiences.

I write about tribal and family history. The voices of my grandmothers can be heard as well as my own, both as a daughter and a mother, set against the backdrop of the prairie and forests of northern Minnesota.

photograph by Ann Mikkelson

Anne M. Dunn

Anne M. Dunn, Anishinabe Ojibwe, was born on the Red Lake Reservation, enrolled on the White Earth Reservation, and for most of her life resided on the Leech Lake Reservation. She has worked for several newspapers and also free-lanced.

Her short stories have been published in three collections: *When Beaver Was Very Grea*t (Midwest Traditions, Inc.), *Grandmother's Gift* and *Winter Thunder* (Holy Cow! Press). A poetry collection, *Uncombed Hair,* was recently published by Loonfeather Press.

Writing is my life now. It is as vital as water, as nourishing as food. Without my pen I am lost. Without paper I am like an old dog looking for a place to die. Although I know that much of what I write will never leave my private pages, I go on writing as though a million people stood waiting for my words.

I am inspired by humanity and loss, by butterflies and birds, old photographs and new shoes.

What is painfully difficult is to discover a place to write. Oh, not just any place and time. What I seek is a writing place with a writer's time.

Ho-wah!

Heid Erdrich

Heid E. Erdrich, Turtle Mountain Ojibwe: Makinak Wajiiwing indoon-jiba, Makwa indodem ganabag. Author of two collections of poems, *The Mother's Tongue* (Salt Press, 2005) and *Fishing for Myth* (New Rivers Press, 1997) co-editor of *Sister Nations* (Minnesota Historical Society Press, 2002); professor at the University of St. Thomas in St. Paul, MN; younger sister of Louise and Lise Erdrich, both writers; raised in Wahpeton, North Dakota where parents taught at the federal Indian boarding school; awards include fellowships from the Bush Foundation, grants from The Loft Literary Center and the State Arts Board as well as Mentor of the Year award from Wordcraft Native Writers in 2004; degrees in writing and literature from Dartmouth and Johns Hopkins as well as an interdisciplinary research doctorate from Union.

꒭

My recent poems have come out of my experience of studying Ojibwe language and learning about the language recovery movement. I decided to use Ojibwe words because speaking them, reading them seems important to their vitality. I've been told by elders that the language is inside us and somehow that seems true: it comes into my dreams so it ends up in my poems. Mistakes in Ojibwe language are mine alone, but they come as sincere attempts to record what has come to me insisting it be spoken. Ojibwe words in my poems are either understood in context or noted below the poem. Some words are the product of dreams and so intentionally not translated or translated imperfectly so as not to offend the spirit of the Ojibwe language.

Louise Erdrich

Louise Erdrich is the author of eleven novels, as well as three volumes of poetry, children's books, and a memoir of early motherhood. Her novel, *Love Medicine,* won the National Book Critics Circle Award and *The Last Report on the Miracles at Little No Horse* was a finalist for the National Book Award in fiction. She grew up in Wahpeton, North Dakota, is German and Ojibwe, and is enrolled in the Turtle Mountain Band of Chippewa. Erdrich founded an independent bookstore, Birchbark Books and Native Arts, in Minneapolis to create a community of encouragement for writers, Native and non-Native, to help writers get read and to bring people together. She lives in Minnesota with her daughters.

I've had a lot of work experiences in my life that make me thankful for what I am doing now. I've hoed sugar beets, lifeguarded, waited tables, I'm certain that having done those jobs helps me as a writer, but I'm very happy to be doing this work now. I write in the morning until I get too tired. I write for as long as I can keep myself awake writing. I fall asleep writing.

I decided to give my time to a writing workshop in the Turtle Mountains, where my mother grew up, because of something I heard from a tribal elder: *when other people tell your story, it always comes out crooked.* It is vital, I think, for Native American People to tell the stories of our own people, in our own voices, from our own perspective. So I've written books that I needed to write. The diversity of people and their experiences in this country absolutely deserves our attention, especially now.

Linda LeGarde Grover

Linda LaGarde Grover is a member of the Bois Forte Band of the Minnesota Chippewa Tribe, wife, mother of three and grandmother of seven. She is a professor in the American Indian Studies Department at the University of Minnesota, Duluth.

In Ojibwe tradition, all that our elders learned from their elders before them combines with their life experiences to become their legacy to the present, and ultimately to the future. We thank them for surviving, we thank them for teaching us by telling their stories and living their lives. We owe it to them to continue the story, past to present, present to future. It is for those who have gone before me that I write; and in keeping with Ojibwe tradition, as I become older it is now also for those of the next generation.

Leslie Harper

Leslie Harper, fiercely Ojibwe, from the Leech Lake Nation. Also called
Daughter, Sister, Auntie, Mom, My Girl. Doesn't photograph well.
Likes a practical, well-running car and good coffee. A competitive yet
compassionate Scrabble player. What I want to do in life: raise my son,
Theo, in a happy and healthy way. I am learning to speak Ojibwe and
it is my son's first language. He is growing up lovingly surrounded by
family and rich in Anishinaabe tradition. I want to think, communicate,
dream and create in ojibwemowin; I want others to, also. Learning
ojibwemowin has strengthened and expanded my understanding of life
in this world. My poetry and stories—my communications—are going
through transformation as I learn our language; it should be interesting
to see where they go.

Harper cavegirl tries to understand the magic box that lights up
words.

Gordon Henry

An Associate Professor of English and American Studies at Michigan State University, Gordon Henry remains rooted in Mt. Pleasant, Michigan. Both poet and novelist, he is an enrolled member of the White Earth Chippewa Tribe of Minnesota. His first novel, *The Light People*, won an American Book Award in 1995 and has recently been reissued from Michigan State University Press. Henry's poetry and fiction is anthologized in various collections including *Songs From This Earth on Turtle's Back, Earth Song, Sky Spirit, Stories Migrating Home, Returning the Gift,* and *Nothing But the Truth.* In 2004, Henry and George Cornell co-authored a middle-school text on the Ojibway for Masoncrest Publishing. He is currently at work on a second novel.

I am engaged in the play of language and meaning as words cross and intersect in different forms. For me storytelling is important because it has the capacity to change, or turn, the consciousness of both the storyteller and the listener. Before the sun turns back, I hope to complete a collaborative work on Turtle Mountain spiritual leader Francis Cree.

Al Hunter

Al Hunter is Anishinaabe from Manitou Rapids, Rainy River First Nations, where he also serves as Chief. His work is featured in the acclaimed anthology, *Days of Obsidian, Days of Grace,* published by Poetry Harbor, Duluth, Minnesota, in 1995. In the summer of 2000, he and his wife, Sandra Indian, led "A Walk To Remember," a 1200 mile sacred journey around Lake Superior "to bring forth community visions of protecting the air, land and water for the Seven Generations yet to come." *Spirit Horses*, his first full-length book of poems, was published by Kegedonce Press in 2001.

When I close my eyes, I can remember the scene behind my house, looking over the rock that sits silently, calmly like a guardian. My mind and heart can remember. And then, there are the trees. The images in my mind of the sun rising visibly beyond the trees, over that standing brother, that old poplar, guardian grandfather, remain vivid and strong. The images in my mind—the trees, this land, the rocks—help me remember not to forget.

Forgetting is easy. It is remembering that is hard. Or is it the forgetting that is hard and the remembering that is easy?

I am remembering the trees, the rocks, the colours, the sky, the snow, the cold, and of the promise of another new day. I am remembering the sun, rising again, a silent magnificent promise of light. Sometimes it's so hard to find the solitude to be able to remember. . . . Sometimes even to forget. Writing is part of this process.

244

Leanne Flett Kruger

Leanne Flett Kruger is Anishnabe/Cree/Metis. She is a graduate of the En'owkin Centre's First Nations Writing School and has published both poetry and fiction. Leanne is Production Manager at Theytus Books, Canada's first and foremost Aboriginal owned and operated publishing company. She is currently working on her first novel, thanks to an Aboriginal Writers Grant awarded by the Canada Arts Council.

Many of my poems were written as class assignments while I attended the En'owkin School of Indigenous Writers. I do not consider myself a poet. I have explored many fields of artistic expression: painting, drawing, writing. I am most comfortable writing fiction but feel it is important to experiment in all genres because it awakens different parts of my creative mind. I love to read Aboriginal poets because if I relate to what a poet is saying, I can feel what I am reading—and Nish poets rock!!

Jamison C. Mahto

I was born in Aberdeen, South Dakota on February 24, 1949 and spent my childhood years growing up in several small towns in northern Minnesota. My grandfather came from the Standing Rock Reservation (Lakota) and my grandmother came from the Red Lake Reservation (Anishinabe). My mother's side of the family came from the Flathead Reservation (Salish-Kootenai) in Montana.

My love for the spoken and written word comes from my father, who, as a high school English teacher, instilled in me the ear to listen to the music of language. I can remember hearing him recite the works of such luminaries as Hermann Hesse, Lawrence Ferlinghetti, and Jack Kerouac, Allen Ginsberg, N. Scott Momaday and, of course, my all-time favorite, Edmund Rostand, author of *Cyrano de Bergerac.*

I graduated with a BA degree in English and Psychology from Macalester College in St. Paul in 1975 where I began dabbling in poetry and reading my work to audiences at the campus coffee house. It was fun and a little crazy but I wasn't really serious. I was more serious about playing rock and roll and have had the experience of playing in accomplished bands. These bands cut records and toured the U.S. I didn't get serious until life had knocked me around a little more, and in 1991-92, because I had a friend who owned a print shop, 2000 copies of *Blues for Franklin Avenue* were printed. I began attending open mic readings and selling copies to those in attendance. It was enough money to keep me in cheeseburgers and fries and moving to the next open mic. I began using copies of this chapbook as a work sample submission for grant applications and based on the artistic merit of the work began receiving grants. All of a sudden, I had a career. Since that time I have published seven works that include a collection of sonnets and an epic poem based on the *Song of Hiawatha* by Longfellow. I am currently working on a novel and a theatrical musical.

I love to play with words. I love that moment when you twist and turn and spit something out that works. A lot of my poetry has been of an experimental nature, some of which works, some of which doesn't. I love the feeling I get when it's rolling. I have never had a block because it goes on all the time.

I once saw the roll of paper on which Kerouac wrote *On the Road.* To be on a roll like that must have been ecstasy. Sometimes I have those moments and I cherish them. To me this is what writing is about. It's me and the blank sheet of paper. It's fun, not work. When it stops being fun and becomes work, that's when I hop on the Harley and ride off into the sunset.

The poem, "The Blue Apache" was written for the quintcentennial de-celebration of the supposed "discovery (?)" of the North American continent. It's Joe, a Native American Viet Nam veteran, standing around the fire with some of the brothers and sisters and he's going to represent. He's going to testify to what the truth is.

The poem, "Litany II" is just that. A prayer of thanks for being able to draw breath and experience life in all of its facets. Like walking in the rain.

Everything is holy. The rocks, clouds, rivers and animals. The stars, sun, moon. People. People and the amazing things we all do. It's all perfection.

You think we can pollute the earth into submission? I doubt it. It's all too beautiful for that. Life and existence will go on. Mother Earth will see to it.

Joyce carlEtta Mandrake

Currently, I live on the Central Oregon Coast with a husband, a son in college, and two cats that live at home. I indulge myself in painting now and then, working on writing children's stories, short stories, poetry, and enjoying reading in between working in the real world. Practicing gratitude on a daily basis is one of my greatest pleasures, particularly watching the sunrise or seeing a double rainbow when driving home from work. Life is good!

I believe that poems are gifts, they grow from unexpected sources, sometimes an idle word from an everyday setting. More often than not, the words that capture us drift in from dreams awake or sleeping. The meaning is always more than just the surface that we see, and if we are lucky we feel the depths of something very deep and old. I grab whatever is available in the moments that I am lucky to receive. As in "Values," a poem comes from life, an idle unthinking speech that left me wondering about manners in the world. "Dream Sequence" is taken from the many vivid dreams that reach me in that wonderful moment between worlds, sleep and waking. "Rest Home" is based upon a visit to a dear friend and how my heart was broken listening to all that was surrounding us.

Rasunah Marsden

A member of Mississaugas of Scugog F.N. & of Anishinabe (Ojibwe) and French ancestry, Rasunah was born in Brandon, Manitoba and obtained teacher training and post-graduate degrees in Fine Arts and Design. She wrote and taught overseas in Brisbane, Jakarta, Perth and Sydney. She then taught creative writing at the Enowkin Centre in Penticton, British Columbia for several years until accepting a position to coordinate the Digital Film & Television program at the Native Education Center in Vancouver, where she and her four grown children reside. Rasunah is a widely anthologized aboriginal writer with several poems featured in *Native Poetry in Canada* (2001) and who edited *Crisp Blue Edges* (2000), a first collection of aboriginal creative non-fiction in North America. Currently she continues as chair and webmaster of the Subud Writer's International (SWI) website.

❦

Funny thing about the absolute lack of recognition of cultural people & works within many first nations, partially because of a natural humility for the work done, partially because there are those who would define what constitutes Indian writing or exert controls over who writes it, & partially because the language of the colonized has been targeted for extinction. Our collections testify that we have come a long way in this area, but dealing death blows to the windigos who would still interpret who we are for us, is a treacherous business. Fortunately, as mentioned by Lee Maracle, "Memory serves." We know who we are. We will write it & they will come.

Rene Meshake

Rene Meshake is an Ojibwe spoken-word performer/singer/song-writer/ player/visual artist living in Guelph, Ontario, Canada. His live shows feature his poems, songs, humour, Ojibwe legends, and anecdotes. Rene's visual art explores the challenges of interpreting the spirit of the legends, music, and the sounds of nature. He draws his strength from his Anishinaabe heritage, specifically his Nookomis whose oral tradition sustains his life and work to this day.

Ever since I could write, I wrote stories. After the betrayal and sexual abuse that I suffered at the Indian Residential School in the early 60s, I wrote no more. But a trip to the Rocky Mountains in 2000 awakened the child in me to write again. I've found writing to be therapeutic. I'm inspired by other survivors of cultural genocide. Social justice issues are connected to my poems. My Ojibwe oral tradition is fully realized in giving spoken-word performances. Each performance piece has led to a step up in my spiritual journey to that place of forgiveness.

Cheryl Minnema

Cheryl Minnema is a member of the Mille Lacs Band of Ojibwe. She was born in Minneapolis, Minnesota and raised on the Mille Lacs Reservation by her mother, Millie Benjamin, and grandmother, Lucy Clark. Graduating from Nay Ah Shing Tribal School as the valedictorian in 1991, she went on to receive her Associate of Arts Degree from Central Lakes Community College and her Bachelor's of Elective Studies from St. Cloud State University. She is a licensed real estate agent, photographer, and Ojibwe craft maker. Cheryl lives in Little Falls, Minnesota with her husband, Ed and two-year-old son, Sean.

I grew up writing poetry, Whether it was to escape, express, or simply create, it became a necessity.

Paulette Molin

Paulette F. Molin, a member of the Minnesota Chippewa Tribe from the White Earth Reservation, is an educator and writer. She has served on the faculty at Hampton University, where her work includes research and writing centered on the institution's historic boarding school program. Her article, "Training the Hand, the Head, and the Heart: Indian Education at Hampton Institute" focuses on early Anishinaabe students and was published in *Minnesota History*. Paulette co-curated the photographic exhibition, *To Lead and To Serve: American Indian Education at Hampton Institute, 1878 to 1923*, which was cosponsored by Hampton University and the Virginia Foundation for the Humanities and Public Policy with support from the National Endowment for the Humanities. More recently, she co-curated *Enduring Legacy: Native Peoples, Native Arts at Hampton,* the permanent American Indian gallery in the Hampton University Museum. Paulette also contributed to *Away from Home: American Indian Boarding School Experiences, 1879-2000,* published in conjunction with the Heard Museum exhibition, *Remembering Our Indian School Days: The Boarding School Experience.* Other work includes co-editing *American Indian Stereotypes in the World of Children,* 2nd edition, with Arlene Hirschfelder and Yvonne Wakim. This publication received the Writer of the Year Award from Wordcraft Circle of Native Writers & Storytellers in 1999. A two-part series, "To Be Examples toTheir People: Standing Rock Sioux Students at Hampton

Institute, 1878-1923," co-authored with Mary Lou Hultgren, was named best article in *North Dakota History Journal* for 2001.

I endeavor to write off some of the weight of colonialist legacies, to lighten the load a bit for all of us carrying that wearisome burden. It means contributing my particular angle of vision and experience to help reclaim Native lives, voices, stories, and histories. Much of my writing has focused on non-fiction, such as boarding school history at Hampton Institute (present-day Hampton University). I see my work as interconnected, part of the larger effort to counter inane stereotypes and hegemonic erasure. Tracing the histories of early students, for instance, reveals names, identities, families, communities and, indeed, nations. These lives, in all their humanity and complexity, belie propagandistic notions and practices that dehumanize and objectify Indian people.

Native writers are very important to me, especially because their words were absent from classroom instruction when I was a young student. Towns bordering reservations, anti-Indian in the main, did not have Native teachers or curricula in their schools. If they had, these two features alone could have made a world of difference to those of us out of the Indian bus. Native writers, now happily too numerous to list here, continue to be sources of inspiration. Among them are the early boarding school students who left traces of themselves in letters, essays, and other writings. Lee Francis, who passed on in 1993, is another. He championed the voices of Native writers and storytellers through his passionate commitment to Wordcraft Circle. I treasure memories of Lee, missing his laughing, funny, bigger-than-life Laguna presence. My family always inspires and sustains me, including my mother whose beauty, strength, and grace are beyond words, my sisters and brothers who pick me up, and other relatives, among them nieces and nephews, who could fill up some buses on their own. Then, too, there is this: that bus to and from the border town is loaded with inspiration, full of lives and stories that need telling.

Jim Northrup

I was born on the Rez, live on the Rez, will probably die on the Rez. T'was a lot that happened in between but it was just details. From those details I make my stories.

I used to be known as a bullshitter but that didn't pay anything so I called myself a storyteller, a little better but it still didn't pay anything. I became a writer, a free lance writer. At the beginning it was more free than lance. But when I became an author and playwright I could charge consultant's fees. Nagaiwanaang niin indoonjibaa. I live with the seasons in what is now called Minnesota.

My relatives, *Nindawemaaganag,* are part of the turning cycle of generations. I am just one of the generations of Anishinaabeg that have lived on this continent. Any author's voice resonates with words, phrases, and events from the past.

One way to find out something is to ask questions. Questions, like family, help make sense of the twists and turns of life. They highlight the humor we're blessed with. They are linguistic twisters; sometimes the shape of the question shifts before you get the answer, then you see the subject in a new way. I'll admit I have a questioning habit.

Lisa Pouport

Lisa M. Poupart (Wabishqeeginuquay) is a member of the Lac Du Flambeau Band of Lake Superior Anishinabe. She is an Associate Professor of Humanistic Studies, American Indian Studies, and Women's Studies at the University of Wisconsin-Green Bay and chairs the American Indian Studies program. Lisa's primary scholarly works are concerned with internalized oppression in American Indian communities and the social problems that stem from this phenomenon including domestic violence, childhood sexual abuse, and delinquency. Her son Skye (Benaisheeanse) is a member of the Oneida Nation of Wisconsin.

Due to ongoing processes of colonization, the oral tradition within many American Indian communities continues to erode. Like other American Indian writers, I use the written word as a form of resistance and reclamation. Over the years, I have filled scores of journals and drawing books with words in an attempt to decolonize my own heart and mind. My written words have carried me through the depths of personal and cultural loss and despair. Today, as a teacher, I draw upon the oral teachings of my elders and the written words of American Indian writers to encourage students to explore and challenge the impacts of colonialism in their own lives.

Marcie Rendon

Marcie R. Rendon is a mother, grandmother, writer and sometimes performance artist. Originally from the White Earth Reservation, she has lived in Minneapolis long enough to not hear the street lights buzz at night.

I write because the words keep coming, ideas grow and characters want to speak.

Armand Garnet Ruffo

Armand Garnet Ruffo is the author of three plays: "Portrait of the Artist As Indian," "A Windigo Tale" (winner of the 2001 CBC Arts Performance Showcase competition) and *Grey Owl: The Mystery of Archie Belaney*.

He is also the author of a collection of poetry, *Opening in the Sky* (1994); a creative biography, *Grey Owl: the Mystery of Archie Belaney* (1997); and most recently, *At Geronimo's Grave*, a collection of poetry (2001). Excerpts from *At Geronimo's Grave* won the 2000 Canadian Authors' Association poetry prize.

Strongly influenced by his Ojibway heritage, his work has appeared in numerous literary journals and anthologies including *Voices of the First Nations* (McGraw-Hill Ryerson, 1996), *Literary Pluralities* (broadview, 1998), *An Anthology of Canadian Native Literature in English* (Oxford, 1998), *Native North America* (ECW, 1999), *An Introduction to Literature* (Nelson, 2000) and *Native Canadian Poetry* (Broadview, 2001).

He is currently the Director of the Centre for Aboriginal Education, Research and Culture, and Assistant Professor in the Department of English, at Carleton University.

My writing is about fostering positive change. I'm saying that to be of Native heritage is something to be proud of, not something to be ashamed of, which has been part and parcel of colonial indoctrination.

While I am certainly occupied with addressing the colonial powers that be and advocating justice for Native people, by no means is all my writing oppositional. I firmly believe that as human beings, as children of the Great Mystery, we all share certain experiences and qualities. Love. Hate. Happiness. Sadness. These things are the emotions and experiences that poets have contemplated since human beings spoke and sang their first words.

Excerpted from *Native Poetry in Canada, A Contemporary Anthology* edited by Jeannette C. Armstrong and Lally Grover. Peterborough, Ontario: Broadview Press, 2000

Denise Sweet

Denise Sweet is a poet, an associate professor at UW-Green Bay, and a creative communications consultant. An Anishinaabe enrolled at White Earth (makwa dodem), she has presented over 200 public readings/performances throughout the U.S., and in Canada, Mexico, Guatemala, and Great Britain. Sweet currently serves as Wisconsin Poet Laureate. She previously served for six years as chair for the American Indian Studies program at Green Bay. She has been the adviser for *Sheepshead Review* and for UWGB's Writer's Union. In 1995, Sweet founded "Who We Are, What Is Ours—A Way With Words," a summer workshop series for young adolescent writers, especially students of color.

Sweet has worked with traditional and contemporary educators in the areas of creativity, diversity, storytelling, drama, and indigenous language preservation. In 1998-99, she coordinated the First Annual Anishinaabeg Symposium on Culture, History and Contemporary Issues, jointly sponsored by UW-Eau Claire and UW-Green Bay. From 1998–2003, she was co-director of the National Native Writers and Artists Forum, and the National Native American Performing Arts Festival, both co-sponsored, in part, by the Navajo Nation and Telluride Institute. In July 1998, she was one of five U.S. writers to attend the 1st World Congress of Indigenous Literatures of the Americas held in Guatemala City, Guatemala.

Denise Sweet's publications include a poetry chapbook, *Know By Heart,* and a collection of poems, *Songs for Discharming* which won the Diane Decorah First Book Award from Native Writers Circle of the

Americas and also won the Posner Award for Poetry from the Wisconsin Council of Writers. She is one of four authors featured in the collections *Days of Obsidian, Days of Grace* and *Nitaawichige: Anishinaabe Poetry and Prose* both from Poetry Harbor Press. Her poetry and fiction have appeared in various anthologies and journals including: *Stories Migrating Home: A Collection of Anishinaabe Prose, Reinventing the Enemy's Language, North American Native Women's Writing, Women Brave in the Face of Danger, Water-Stone Review, Wisconsin Academy Review, Another Chicago Magazine, North Coast Review, Cream City Review* and *Plainswoman.*

Sweet has been the recipient of a Literary Arts Fellowship from the Wisconsin Arts Board. She has a completed manuscript, *As Those With Faith Will Do: Selected Poetry and Prose,* and her current work-in-progress is a collection of short prose and performance poems, *Travelling: The Up North Poems.*

Her proudest achievements, however, are as mother and grandmother. Her sons, Damon and Vaughn, ages 29 and 27, are two fine Anishinaabeg men (migizi dodem). She is also inspired by and supremely devoted to her grandchildren, Jasmine, Bazile, and Sophie.

❧

Native people have always felt and respected the power of words, the beauty of great oratory, and the fierce pride of knowing that a language belongs to them and they to it. The language of poetry is no less sacred and, for me, holds the same power and beauty.

I pay homage to that gift every time I read or write a poem. Poetry is about the miracle of language. And miracles still happen all the time in this world.

Mark Turcotte

Mark Turcotte (Turtle Mountain Ojibwe) is the author of four poetry collections, including *Exploding Chippewas* (2002). Recipient of 1999 and 2003 Wisconsin Arts Board Literary Fellowships, he was also selected for a 2001-02 Lannan Foundation Literary Grant. He recently completed a Lannan Writer's Residency in Marfa, Texas, and an American Voices assignment for the National Book Foundation in Wind River, Wyoming. He now lives and works out of Chicago and Kalamazoo, where he is participating in the MFA Program at Western Michigan University.

I like to write about moments, watching them expand into something larger, maybe even timeless.

Doyle Turner, Jr.

I grew up in Naytahwaush, at the center of the White Earth Indian reservation in the northwestern part of Minnesota. I am an enrolled member of the Mississippi band of the White Earth nation. The lakes and woods are beautiful there and littered with story after story of my family. When I was twelve years old, my family moved to Chicago, Illinois, and I discovered writing was a powerful tool for reliving and reconnecting to the place where my heart still resided. I was lucky enough to find an English teacher there who encouraged my heart-sore reminiscence.

I continued to favor the writing and study of literature (stories) inherent in English, earning a B.A. in English from Moorhead State University, and returned to the White Earth reservation to work in the public schools for three years. Inspired by great teachers, I returned to Moorhead State University and earned a B.S. in English Education.

I have taught stories and writing to seventh grade students in the Bemidji Public Schools for the past eleven years in Bemidji, Minnesota, earning an M.S. in English Education through Bemidji State University. Bemidji is where I live with my wife, Molly, and my two children, Tony and Sophia.

I try to connect what I write to the natural world. I grew up with a wonderful grandfather, Tony Turner. He knew about the woods and I was lucky enough to spend a lot of time with him in the outdoors. He was also a master storyteller, and what I know about the sacredness of story, I've learned from him. I find the truth of my experience through close examination of the images and the sounds of the woods, my remembrances, and the stories my grandfather told. It is my grandfather nestled inside my history which is part and parcel of my sense of place, the land where I grew up, which now lives in my own stories.

I enjoy exploring rhythm, surprise, and playing with the tricks of language in what I write.

Turtle Heart

Turtle Heart's father was an Ahnishinabek man of the White Earth Band of the River Otter Clan of the Ahnishinabeg people. His father was a career military officer and this had the family traveling all over the world, rather than his spending a childhood on the reservation. Turtle Heart is a Viet Nam era veteran. For some years he was involved in modern medicine at the emergency room and trauma levels. In recent years he has moved closer and closer to what he sees as the center of the will and intent of his tribal elders. Through stone sculpture and paintings Turtle Heart makes his living. On the Internet, his website (www.aicap.org) was one of the first Native American web spaces to come online. His work was archived in the Permanent Collection of the Smithsonian in 1997. Turtle Heart travels extensively and shares his songs, poetry and sculptures. For many years he has had a small gallery and studio in Taos. He has traveled and spoken extensively on the philosophy of tribal religion and culture. Turtle Heart is also a pioneer in digital art and is the first Native American to have digitally-created paintings exhibited worldwide and published online. His work is in numerous corporate, government, and private art collections worldwide. Discovering and experiencing the wide travels and world experience of the Ahnishinabe people has been a source of great surprise and happiness for the artist. Currently the author lives and works on a tiny island called Pantelleria in the Mediterranean Sea, a part of Sicily.

When I live with and work to understand my songs and poems I feel close to the living spirit and soul of my Ahnishinabeg ancestors, to the earth and to the mystery of life. When I am able to share my songs and poems with others I have seen and felt the gentle and loving healing touch they have on all of our hearts. I am satisfied that my poems are the living line between my life at this moment and the sacred hearts of those sacred tree people who brought me this life and this moment. These poems are stated in the formal rhythms of the sacred societies and come from the consciousness of the natural clans which brought my culture so much healing and learning powers and blessings. We sometimes call these poems "acts of consciousness," as they represent a willing awareness of what the spirit teachers expect from us when we study and think about the sacred.

E. Donald Two-Rivers

Eddy Two-Rivers is an accomplished poet, novelist and playwright and is the recipient of the prestigious 1999 American Book Award. A theatrical pioneer, he founded the Red Path Theater Company, the only Native American theater company in Illinois.

An enrolled member of the Seine River band of Ojibwe Indians in Northwestern Ontario, Two-Rivers is a tireless activist for Native Americans, Mother Earth, and the civil rights of all people. His dedication to these causes earned him the distinguished Iron-Eyes Cody Award for Peace in 1992. His writing has remained deeply rooted in these plights.

As a teen in the politically turbulent 60s, he relocated to Chicago, spending his youth in rebellious exploration of a life as a Native American in Urban America. His first-hand experience with the negative results of mixing violence and activism led him to eventually lower his fist and pick up a pen, channeling his passion for the rights of his Native American community onto paper.

Since then, Two-Rivers has authored a screenplay, a collection of plays entitled *Briefcase Warriors,* a short story collection which won the American Book Award, *Survivor's Medicine,* and two collections of poems: *A Dozen Cold Ones* and *Pow-Wows, Fat Cats, and Other Indian Tales.* In all of these works, he recognizes the struggle of all people, including whites, Hispanics, Blacks, Asians, and of course, Native Americans, against impoverishment, racism and injustice. Publisher's Weekly says, "One senses that this is one storyteller who knows whereof he speaks."

Poetry is like a magnifying glass—a tool to inspect the point of intersection where the roads of experience converge to form an idea, a value. In writing poetry for publication, your fundamental being is laid open, your intimacy with yourself shattered, but that's okay.

Through my poetry I hope to be recognized as a product of the land—a child of the Anishanobae Nation, one of the Ozhkabewisug—the messengers. Through my poetry I want my words to speak of the spiritual relationship between humans and the rest of life on this earth. I want my voice to join my relatives of all nations who are speaking of solutions and requesting respect for Mother Earth.

Gerald Vizenor

Gerald Vizenor is Professor Emeritus of American Studies at the University of California, Berkeley and a Professor of American Studies at the University of New Mexico. He is the author of more than twenty books on Native histories, critical studies, and original literature, including *The People Named the Chippewa, Manifest Manners: Narratives on Postindian Survivance,* and *Native States of Literary Sovereignty.*

His third novel, *Griever: An American Monkey King in China,* won the American Book Award. His most recent books include *Hotline Healers: An Almost Browne Novel, Fugitive Poses: Native American Scenes of Absence and Presence, Chancers,* a novel, and two books of original Haiku, *Raising the Moon Vines* and *Cranes Arise. Hiroshima Bugi: Atomu 57* is his most recent novel. *Bear Island: The War at Sugar Point,* a narrative poem, is forthcoming from University of Minnesota Press.

Gerald Vizenor is series editor of American Indian Literature and Critical Studies at the University of Oklahoma Press. He is an enrolled member of the Minnesota Chippewa Tribe, White Earth Reservation.

I write to create imagic and ironic scenes, to create original metaphors of nature, to tease the obvious, and to liberate words from mundane histories and cultural simulations.